To

_____

From

_____

Date

_____

# EXTRAORDINARY WONDERS

*More Than Coincidence . . .*
*True Stories of God's Miracles in Everyday Life*

**Guideposts**

New York

# MYSTERIOUS WAYS: EXTRAORDINARY WONDERS

ISBN-10: 0-8249-3214-5
ISBN-13: 978-0-8249-3214-5

Published by Guideposts
16 East 34th Street
New York, New York 10016
Guideposts.org

Distributed by Ideals Publications, a Guideposts company
2630 Elm Hill Pike, Suite 100
Nashville, Tennessee 37214

## Acknowledgments

Scripture references are from the following sources: The Holy Bible, New International Version®, NIV®. Copyright © 1973, 1978, 1984, 2011 by Biblica, Inc.™ Used by permission of Zondervan. All rights reserved worldwide. The New American Standard Bible® (NAS), Copyright © 1960, 1962, 1963, 1968, 1971, 1972, 1973, 1975, 1977, 1995 by The Lockman Foundation. Used by permission.

Cover and interior design by Jeff Jansen/Aesthetic Soup | www.aestheticsoup.net
Cover photo © Nick | 2056 | Dreamstime.com
Typeset by Aptara, Inc.

Printed and bound in China
10 9 8 7 6 5 4 3 2 1

# Contents

# Contents

# Contents

# INTRODUCTION

*I* have lived, sir, a long time, and the longer I live, the more convincing proofs I see of this truth—that God governs in the affairs of men."

These words by Benjamin Franklin express well the Christian's view of God and life. God is intricately involved in the affairs of this world, and He is intricately involved in the affairs of your life. He cares about the big, and He cares about the small.

While we occasionally think of ourselves as living *under* God, and by extension, separate from Him, intermittently we get the sense that we are living *with* Our Creator—that He takes a special interest in us, answers our prayers, listens to our needs, and fortifies our resolve.

In the true stories you are about to read, you will see God stepping in and entering the lives of ordinary men and women. Experience with them *Extraordinary Wonders*. You will be astounded as you witness God redeeming, managing, and providing to reassure, protect, and work recovery for His people. We hope sincerely that your faith will be strengthened in return.

# 1

# *E*XTRAORDINARY
# *P*ROVIDENCE

*A*re not two sparrows sold for a penny? Yet not one
of them will fall to the ground outside your Father's
care. And even the very hairs of your head are all
numbered."

MATTHEW 10:29–30 NIV

———————— ✺ ————————

*Oh, Lord, thank You for caring for Your children so tenderly
and working miracles in our lives.*

# My Lena

## by Christine West

———

Grandma, Grandma, tell us a story!" Four darling children sat by my feet, looking up at me expectantly.

Suddenly, we were interrupted by clapping. "Terrific," the director said, stepping up to the stage from the chapel aisle. "Except, could you kids face the audience a bit more?" The kids shifted to face the empty pews, which would be filled in a few days for the church play. "Perfect," the director said. "Now, Grandma, read to your grandchildren." A pang of sadness hit me. If only I could read to my real grandchild!

I had a granddaughter, but I'd never met her. Sixteen years earlier my son was involved in a relationship that ended badly. But out of it came a blessing: a baby girl named Lena. I yearned to be a grandmother to her—but shortly after the birth, the mother moved and left no forwarding address. My son had no idea where his daughter was. Over the years, I asked around town to try and find my son's ex, but it seemed she didn't want to be found.

I'd just joined this new church a week earlier, and was promptly offered the part of Grandma in the play. At least now I could pretend to be a grandma. The rehearsals went well, and finally the day of the show arrived. The performance was great. "You all looked so natural up there," one of my friends said.

Afterward, we went to the church basement for refreshments. I walked over to one of the girls in the play. Rehearsals had been such a whirlwind we never really got to talk. "How's my granddaughter?" I joked.

"Fine!" she answered. Just then, someone else walked up and asked the girl her name.

I wasn't sure I heard the girl's answer correctly. But it made me ask her another question. "What's your mother's name?"

She told me.

I was still in shock. "And what's your father's name?" I asked.

It was my son.

"Lena," I said, "you're not going to believe this . . . but, I really *am* your grandmother!"

She'd only started going to that church a week before I did. Since that day of the play, we've stayed close. Not long ago, she even made me a great-grandma.

# Stranded in a Snowbank

*by Vishnu "Chuck" Mulay, MD*

---

There are a lot of lessons a young surgeon learns. One of the biggest to come my way happened outside the operating room in the dead of winter many years ago.

Back then I was practicing at a small hospital in Manchester, Iowa, about nineteen miles west of my home in Dyersville. An easy half-hour drive on a two-lane country road. Easy in good weather, that is. I had a hernia surgery scheduled at seven thirty one morning. The patient was a young boy. The surgery didn't worry me so much, but the weather did. I looked out my window before I went to sleep the night before. Snow was coating the trees in our neighborhood. The road was almost completely white. *Hope I can get to the hospital tomorrow*, I thought, vowing to get an extra-early start.

First thing in the morning, I looked out the window again. The snow had slowed. *I can make it*, I thought. I dressed, threw on my coat, and hopped in the car.

The road was icy but manageable. Then, halfway to the hospital, the tires lost their grip. I tried to steer, but the car just slid . . . right off the road. *Bam!* White burst across the windshield. I'd ditched into a huge snowbank.

Shaken, I got out of the car, pulling my coat tight. The temperature was below zero, and the light snow had become a full-blown blizzard. I looked around. No cars in either direction. Not at this hour, not in this weather. The closest town was miles away. I'd succumb to hypothermia before I got anywhere. For the first time in my adult life, I was truly terrified. *God, if You really are there, I could use some help.*

Just then, I saw headlights in the distance. A four-wheel-drive Scout. I waved frantically. The vehicle pulled over. Inside was an elderly farm couple. "Need a ride?" the man asked. His wife offered me a cup of coffee from their thermos.

"Thank you so much," I said, climbing into the backseat of the Scout.

"What are you doing on the road in this weather?" the woman asked.

"I'm a doctor," I said, "and I'm headed to the hospital in Manchester."

"So are we!" said the man. "Our grandson is having surgery today. Maybe you know the surgeon. His name is Dr. Mulay."

# A Place to Rest My Head

*by Diane E. Robertson*

My lupus had flared up and I was in terrible pain. The doctor had put me on a powerful anti-inflammatory medications. Still, I could barely walk. My husband, Sal, was overseas on business and my parents lived a thousand miles away. "Come on home," my dad said. "We'll take care of you." Mom's chicken soup and a warm bed sounded like the perfect cure. Now I just had to get through the flight there.

A friend drove me to the airport and dropped me at the curb. I stepped out of the car. Pain shot through my lower back. I winced. "Are you okay?" my friend asked. "Sure," I said, not wanting to worry her. The skycap offered me a wheelchair, but I wasn't comfortable sitting. Maybe it would be easier to walk to the gate.

"Your flight's been delayed for an hour," the sky-cap said. An hour? Another hour of agony. I walked slowly through the terminal. *God*, I prayed, *I need a place to lie down for an hour. Some place to rest.*

That's when I saw the ladies' room. *If I splash some water on my face, I'll feel better*, I thought. Imagine my surprise when I stepped inside and saw an old-fashioned lounge area with a long mirror, a dressing table, and a couch. I sank down. The last thing I saw before I closed my eyes was a bit of graffiti on the opposite wall that read, "I love Jimmy."

An hour's rest on that couch, and I was able to make it to my parents'. Ten days of bed rest under their care helped immensely. I flew home in much better shape and Sal picked me up at the airport. Walking down the terminal, I was going to tell him about the couch when we came to that same ladies' room. "Excuse me for a moment," I said.

I darted in. There was the long mirror, the dressing table, even that familiar bit of graffiti: "I love Jimmy." But no couch. An attendant was cleaning so I asked if she'd changed things around. "No, no," she replied. The lounge had always been set up this way.

There had never been a couch in there. Except the one hour when I desperately needed it.

# Not by Bread Alone...

*by Margaret Rudkin*

———— ⁂ ————

*T*here's an old Irish saying: "God broadens the back to bear the burden." Grandmother used to quote this proverb each time we launched some new project. "You children have talent," she would say. "Don't be afraid to step out. You won't be alone."

I never had to learn exactly what Grandmother meant until the day my husband, Henry, and I first heard low, gurgling sounds come from our son's chest. The child had asthma: We were on the threshold of needing broader backs than we had ever imagined necessary.

For seven years Henry and I went through torture, listening to this little boy struggle for breath during the attacks. We spent half our time following doctors' instructions, but there seemed to be nothing we could do except pray.

Finally, we made rules for ourselves: no more doctors, no more "cures." But, of course, that didn't work.

When your child can't breathe, you grasp at anything. Then, one afternoon, a friend came to our Connecticut farm and told us of a famous doctor who had gotten results in allergy cases with a high-protein diet.

"Why don't you drop in and see him?" she suggested. "Tell him I sent you. It can't do any harm."

This doctor's theory was that man is harmed by his own blundering treatment of natural foods. Our bodies are often starved for lack of right food values, such as is found in stone-ground whole-wheat flour. I went home and boldly announced that I was going to buy some real whole wheat, and bake my son a loaf of bread.

Now, I'd never made bread in my life, but in the kitchen I struggled to reproduce an old-fashioned homemade loaf. All the old cookbook recipes had a long list of ingredients: whole-wheat flour (stone ground); pure honey; fresh, whole dairy milk; pure butter; and so forth. "Nobody makes bread with these anymore," I said to myself. But I decided to use them all.

The noise of clanging utensils that followed must have sounded like a battery of bakers at work. Not knowing what I was doing, I made a dough and stuck it in the oven. An hour later I took out my first loaf of bread.

It was awful.

On the outside it was crooked; it sank low in the middle, and was about as solid as a brick. When I put it on the table, I could see my family choke. It took weeks of repeated trial and error—still not knowing what I was doing—before at last I produced a loaf that caused Henry to sit back, his eyes bright, and say: "Now that's bread."

Slowly, with his new diet, my son's wheezing and coughing lessened, and the child grew stronger. I certainly do not want to say it was my home-baked bread that cured my son of asthma. There was another factor working: strange "coincidences" that I seemed to have no control over. The development of this first successful loaf into Pepperidge Farm bread was to come about through a chain of such unusual coincidences that I hesitate to use the word. Some people would call them "accidents." I like to think that God and prayer work through people in remarkable ways.

For instance, many friends, tasting my bread, began to suggest that I put it on the market. A few days later, I made eight loaves of bread, then took them down to a local grocer.

"I would like you to taste a piece of bread," I said, and happened upon a very successful sales technique. The grocer's face brightened. Three hours later he telephoned me excitedly that the bread was already sold out and asked for a regular supply.

Although I knew nothing of manufacturing, of marketing, of pricing, or of making bread in quantities, with that phone call Pepperidge Farm bread was born.

One evening Henry casually mentioned that he was helping a fund-raising campaign for the Visiting Nurses. He told me the story of Lillian Wald, a wealthy Jewish woman, who was devoting her life to service for others, through her nursing program.

"I'd love to meet this woman," I remarked, but knowing how busy her life was, I never dreamed it would be possible. About a year later I was out for a drive when my car broke down, "accidentally." From a large house nearby a chauffeur appeared and personally did the repair work. He would accept nothing for his trouble.

"Surely there's some way I can thank you," I said.

"It was my employer sent me down, ma'am. Miss Wald."

Taking the opportunity, I walked up to the house, rang the bell, and met Lillian Wald. We became close friends. It was she who inspired me to think of my bread-making as both an enterprise and a form of service to others.

Perhaps it is through such "coincidences" (our son's illness, inventing our bread recipe, friends suggesting making bread en masse, and now the meeting with Miss Wald), perhaps through these "accidents," God broadens our backs to do work we never dream lies within our capabilities.

Certainly, the problems that arose seemed beyond my capabilities. First, as the demand for our bread increased, we had to get stone-ground flour in large quantities. Almost all the stone grinding mills disappeared decades ago. We even considered setting up our own mill, but that would have required thousands of dollars and I was determined to let all new equipment come from profits. Yet there could be no profits without flour.

One day, by chance, we heard from an acquaintance this completely casual remark: "You know, there's a man up in Connecticut who has an interesting hobby. Has an old-fashioned stone mill. Grinds his own flour."

My husband and I rushed up to meet him and discovered a mill that had ground flour since Revolutionary days. I explained my project.

"You realize, of course, that my mill is just a hobby," the gentleman said. That was the problem. None of us knew anything about milling; the art of the stone mill had been almost lost. We went ahead, though, using his flour, knowing we were doing many things wrong for lack of technical knowledge.

Somehow we expanded, moving our pots and pans from the kitchen to the stables. Then, one day a woman reporter was sent out to the farm to do a story on us. Later she called me at my office in the stable.

"Mrs. Rudkin, I'm down at an old secondhand bookstore. I just happened to run across a book you might be interested in."

It was an old, technical volume about stone milling. It turned out to be the bible of the trade—and had all the answers we needed to operate the old stone mill.

This last event drew my husband into the business. Henry had always taken my commercial bread-making somewhat as a joke. Now, through the technical side of the business, he became greatly interested.

"You know, our stones aren't far enough apart," he would say. "We've got to do something about that. It says here you can burn your wheat if the stones aren't properly set." Out came his calipers and measuring tapes.

Henry today is one of the outstanding milling experts in America. Bit by bit he began turning his full time away from Wall Street toward making bread.

Henry at first laughed at the way I kept books. He would walk into the stable and see me scribbling on little scraps of paper. This was my bookkeeping: so much in, so much out; the rest was profit.

Now his attitude changed. "Anyone who puts out a thousand loaves of bread a day is in business, Peg. Let's set up a regular bookkeeping system so you'll know where you stand."

A thousand loaves of bread a day. Then four thousand . . . ten thousand. We moved from the stables to an abandoned gas station. Then we had to build a new plant, specially designed for hand-kneaded bread.

As we increased production, we were, of course, faced with difficulties keeping the home-made quality. Yet we've done it. When I was invited to give a lecture before a group of manufacturers, I said, "We succeeded at Pepperidge Farm by breaking all the rules of manufacturing." We have kept each of the theories of bread-making we started with in the kitchen of our farmhouse.

This means extra help, no rigid standardizations, and family relationship with every employee.

Fourteen years after I rattled and clanged my way through that first loaf of bread, we were producing thousands of loaves a day: whole wheat and white. We had three bakeries, four mills, over one hundred employees. Our bread has been eaten, literally, half the world over.

If, as I worked over that first soggy loaf, I had seen the modern bakery, I would have said, "That's impossible. It belongs to someone else." I didn't realize that you walk a mile by taking one step at a time.

Grandmother's first words to us, "Don't be afraid to step out," have come to a fuller meaning. We know, now, not to be afraid to get started on some new venture just because the end of the mile seems so far away. We don't worry about the end of the mile—we just take the first step. God will broaden the back to bear the burden.

# THREE MYSTERY BASKETS

*by Phyllis J. Agness*

— ∰ —

$M$y office at the college was filled with Easter baskets that Good Friday morning. I'm a professor at the
Indiana University-Purdue University Fort Wayne
campus, and every year I do a volunteer project with
my students—they put together Easter baskets for the
homeless children and their moms at our local shelters. Each basket is unique, specially created and personalized for a woman or a child, and each bears the
name of the person receiving it.

Proud of the work my students had done, I carefully
checked the baskets against my list. Then my husband,
Tom, and I loaded them into our van and delivered
them to the appropriate shelters. At each and every
stop I checked my list again. All one hundred baskets
were accounted for. Mission accomplished.

I returned to my office later that morning. I
opened the door and gasped. There, on my desk,

were three more baskets. I inspected them closely, but they had no names on them.

*Now where did these come from?* I wondered.

I went over my list again and called the shelters. No one was missing a basket. I took the three baskets home and showed them to Tom. "What will we do with them?" I asked.

"Maybe we could hand them out on the street," he suggested.

"But they're probably meant for someone specific," I said.

All Saturday I worried about it. I didn't want someone to feel left out. Then that night I got an urgent call from one of the shelters.

"Phyllis, I know this is late notice, but we just had another family come in. Do you have any baskets left over?"

"How many do you need?" I asked.

"Three. For a mother, her ten-year-old son, and her six-year-old daughter."

I turned to the baskets. One had a kite, perfect for a ten-year-old boy; another had hair ribbons, just right for a young girl; and the last had shampoo, stockings, lipstick, and a mirror. Seems there another list even more accurate than mine.

# KINSEY

*by Rhonda Vecera Naylor*

My paternal grandmother, who immigrated to this country from Czechoslovakia, died when I was eighteen. I missed her, especially at the big events in my life such as my marriage and the birth of my first child. I often caught myself thinking back to Nanny's cozy kitchen; she let me help her roll out dough for pastries and strudels while regaling me with tales of her Old World girlhood. Though her jumbled English translations of Czech phrases were often stumbling blocks, I always knew Nanny loved me.

When we had our second daughter, my husband, Ronny, decided he didn't like the name we had agreed on months earlier. I was taken aback by his abrupt change. On the day I was to come home from the hospital, we still hadn't picked a name! I wished Nanny were here. *God*, I finally prayed, *help us get over this stumbling block and find the perfect name.*

We named the baby Kinsey, a name Ronny liked. I had a hard time getting used to it, and often wondered during that first year if I ever would. Then one day we got a letter from my mom, containing the death certificate of my dad's brother. Mom had drawn an arrow pointing to the space where my grandma's maiden name was listed. I had only known her Czech last name: Komina. Now I gazed in wonderment at the English version—Kinsey.

Every day now when I look into Kinsey's cheery face I see a godly reminder of my grandmother's lasting love.

# Gifts for the Children

*by Peggy King*

———— ⁄⁄⁄ ————

The phone rang as I was pulling my elf hat out of the closet. Every December my husband, Jerry, and I help the Lions Club deliver presents to the forty students of a nearby residential school for kids with special needs. Tomorrow everyone would gather at the local firehouse, and in addition to "Santa" and his "elf," there'd be a magic show and a buffet lunch. The kids would even get a firehouse tour. I couldn't wait.

But on the other end of the phone was a distressed volunteer. "Peggy, we've got a big problem," she said. "We just found out there are sixty kids coming this year."

Sixty! We only had forty presents to give! We had no more money, and no time to find donations. I looked at Jerry. "We need the real Santa Claus," I said.

The next day, Jerry and I drove to the firehouse dejected. We parked the same time as another car. The driver, a tall man, got out and walked alongside us to the building. There was something impressive in the way he carried himself. He wasn't a fireman or a volunteer I recognized. Maybe a parent of one of the kids?

We reached the front door and the man looked confused. "Isn't the vote here today?" he asked me. I knew there was a referendum up for a vote in our town—but it wasn't being held here.

"Not at this firehouse," I answered.

The man shook his head. "I don't usually get these things wrong," he said. "I don't know how I could have been mistaken." He looked at Jerry and me. "Why are you here?"

"A Christmas party, for special-needs kids . . . or at least that was the plan . . ." I trailed off. He seemed nice, but I was too worried to chitchat. I quickly blurted out our dilemma.

"How many toys do you need?" the man asked. I told him and he took off in his car, promising to be back as soon as he could.

Minutes before the children arrived, the man burst through the door—his arms overflowing with bags of toys.

We needed a Santa Claus. We were sent Major Tom Quigley—leader of the local Marine Toys for Tots program, who had plenty of presents on hand to help give every last child an unforgettable Christmas.

# A Future and a Hope

*by Ann-Marie Walker*

---

$\mathcal{T}$wice a year Gary and I took the kids and made the 1,200-mile trip up from Alabama to my native New England to visit my folks, crowding into their cozy little house on Cape Cod. I loved those trips. One year my daughter, Michelle, gave me a ceramic cottage that looked like one of the saltboxes on the Cape, with cedar trees on either side and a quaint old rowboat out front. "So you can feel close even when you're in Alabama," she said. I gave Michelle a big kiss and a hug in return.

We all got older. I worried about Mom's worsening diabetes. Dad had a heart attack. Suddenly, they were facing a move to the nursing home.

"I can't let that happen," I told Gary.

"Let's move up north and take care of your parents," he said. Our kids were grown by then. It was possible.

We put our things in storage and moved into my parents' basement on Cape Cod, but it wasn't quite the same. The vacation cottage was way too small for the four of us to live there full time.

Gary and I had to find a place of our own. The houses we saw were too expensive or too far from my parents. I tried to take comfort in my favorite Scripture, from Jeremiah (29:11 NIV): "For I know the plans I have for you . . . plans to prosper you and not to harm you, to give you hope and a future." But the longer we looked, the more I wondered what lay ahead for us. For my parents.

One summer day the Realtor showed us a saltbox house down the road from Mom and Dad's. It was lovely. Even better, I had a tremendously warm feeling about it, like those old vacations. I couldn't explain it.

What a relief to finally unpack our things! They'd been in storage so long, it was like seeing them for the very first time. Except when I unwrapped the ceramic cottage my daughter gave me. I turned it over in my hands. The sloping roof, the shutters . . . it was an exact replica of our new house, right down to the cedars and the quaint rowboat the previous owners had left on the lawn. A future and a hope. It had been there all along.

# Dreaming of Baby

*by Katy Brown*

············ —◆— ············

$\mathcal{T}$he hot summer days seemed to crawl by. My husband and I were waiting for our county adoption agency to complete the long process of clearing us so we could adopt a baby. We'd already gone through months of being interviewed and investigated—and we were told we would have another long wait even after we were approved.

Early one July morning, before dawn, I was startled awake by a vivid dream about a baby. What a happy dream that was—surely we'd have our baby soon!

But August passed without any developments, and September came before we even received our letter of clearance. Still, though our "credentials" were established, nothing happened. September dragged into October, and then November plodded by.

At last, two weeks before Christmas, the telephone call came. A woman at the adoption agency told me that the mother of a baby girl had reviewed the records of people who wanted to become adoptive parents and had chosen us. She gave me various details about the baby's birth and made an appointment for my husband and me to see her.

I hung up the phone and got out my desk calendar to mark the date and time. Riffling through the pages, I saw a notation in my handwriting.

A prickle ran up my spine.

On the calendar page for July 20, I'd written "dreamed about baby."

That was the very day God had chosen for our adopted daughter to be born.

# DELAYED!

*by Debra Davis*

---

$\mathcal{T}$he woman at the airline ticket counter in Munich, Germany, just shook her head. "I'm sorry, but there's no more availability on this flight," she said. *Great*, I thought. My husband, Bob, and I had enjoyed every moment of our dream vacation, two weeks in Europe, but I was ready to go home to Shreveport, Louisiana, and sleep in my own bed. Bob could see how frustrated I was. "We'll just have to try to get on the flight tomorrow," he said. "Let's enjoy the extra day."

*Bob's right*, I thought. There were more important things to be worried about—my son Joe, a first lieutenant in the Army 82nd Airborne Division, would be returning to Fort Bragg in North Carolina for a short R & R from his tour of duty in Baghdad, and we weren't sure we'd be able to see him in the little time he'd be stateside. Plus the time was so up in the air! Back at our hotel, I checked my e-mail to see if our daughter-in-law, Monica, had any news on when Joe was due to arrive. Sure enough, there was a message. "Joe's been delayed again," it read, with one of those little frowny faces.

The next morning we made it onto our flight back to the States. Unfortunately, we had to stop in Atlanta. Our connecting flight there was delayed because of bad weather. The hours passed. I felt the frustration building. "That's it!" I finally said. "I just want to get home already!"

That's when I saw a group of soldiers coming down the ramp from one of the gates. I thought of Joe. *They're coming back from a war*, I reminded myself. *I'm coming back from vacation. What right do I have to be frustrated?* Maybe the troops were God's way of reminding me to trust in His time. Bob grabbed my arm. "Look at those soldiers coming down the ramp."

"I see them," I said. Bob persisted. "Do you see who's in front?" Suddenly, all those delays across all those miles made perfect sense. I rushed toward my son Joe's open arms.

# A Cake for Lewis

*by Abbie Daigle*

*I* was spending a year working and living at the St. Francis Inn, a soup kitchen and an outreach to the homeless on the east side of Philadelphia. It was in the Kensington neighborhood, an area so rough that the police nicknamed it "The Badlands"—abandoned houses, prostitution, drugs, poverty. The landscape was bleak and depressing. Which was just why I had to move there. I wanted to help people caught up in such circumstances.

One of my duties as a volunteer at the Inn was to drive a van from supermarket to supermarket, collecting much of their donated food. We got all kinds of things, from canned goods to day-old rolls. And we put everything to good use.

But one day last fall I picked up something that made me feel so sad. It was a beautiful birthday cake, with blue and yellow frosting on top. "Happy Birthday,

Lewis," read the bright script on top. *Poor kid never got his birthday cake*, I thought. I put the cake in the van, said a quick prayer for Lewis (whoever he was, wherever he was), and finished up my rounds.

Back at the Inn, I stacked the birthday cake up with the other food we would be distributing.

Later that afternoon I was back at the Inn, sorting mail in the office, when Sister Janette walked in, wearing a triumphant smile and carrying the cake in her arms. "Look what came in today!" she exclaimed. "It's a birthday cake! Can you believe it?"

Sister Janette worked with the neighborhood children. She reminded me about the mother who had called her the other day, asking if there was any way she could get something for her little boy to take to school to help celebrate his birthday. Like most families who came to St. Francis Inn, they had nothing.

"Perfect," I said. Or almost. Well, maybe we could scrape off the name that was on the cake.

Sister Janette opened the lid of the box to take a look. "Oh my!" she said, gasping. "My little Lewis is going to be so happy!"

# MIA

### by Holly Funk

--- ~ ---

*T*wins. Ever since my husband, Doug, and I chose to adopt, we requested twin girls. I felt that God meant for us to have twins—the number "two" just wouldn't leave my head. We bought a tandem stroller, baby blankets, even two little wind-up lambies that played music. But then an adoption agency introduced us to a thirteen-month-old girl who had been abandoned outside a textile factory in Yangzhou, China.

Doug and I fell in love with her instantly, and all thoughts of twins were put aside. I knew we had to name her Mia. I had never considered that name before, but somehow it just seemed right (and by now maybe you've noticed that I'm often at the mercy of God's little "nudges").

In July 2004, we brought baby Mia home with us to Chicago. We gave away the tandem stroller and extra blanket and bought a single stroller, but for some reason I couldn't part with that second little lambie.

There was an Internet forum for parents who had adopted from the same orphanage. For a year I shared updates on Mia's progress.

Then one day I noticed a posting from a woman named Diana in Florida who was talking about her daughter, a little girl who was the same age as Mia. I sent her an e-mail and she answered me right away.

Her daughter's birthday was the same as Mia's. "Where was Mia found?" she asked me. Turned out both girls were found in the very same place, a week apart.

We exchanged pictures. Wow! The girls looked so much alike! So many similarities. Could it be? Only a DNA test could tell us for sure. So Diana and I did a swab test on our daughters. The girls were related all right . . . they were twins!

Our daughters met for the first time last August. They hugged each other and acted almost as if they had never been apart. Mia gave her sister the lambie that was meant especially for her.

Oh, and there is one other thing that the two girls have in common. There's not just one Mia. Her twin is named Mia too.

# The Hitchhikers

*by Ray Cripps*

············ ⸏⸏⸏ ············

*I*'d like it to be a vacation that God could use," said my wife, Jean, the night before we set off to tour Scotland three summers ago. It was the first time in twenty years we had been able to plan a break for just the two of us. Dave and Pete, our two sons, were camping in France, while our thirteen-year-old daughter, Mary, had just gone on a hiking trip with the Girl Guides.

So it was with light and thankful hearts that we piled our luggage into our old Morris and set off, in glorious sunshine, up to the M5 and M6, two of Britain's motorways, on the first leg of the long journey to the north.

The roads became more congested the farther north we went, and we began to notice numbers of youngsters standing at the roadside, waiting hopefully for lifts. Although British drivers have had fewer bad experiences with hitchhikers than Americans, my wife and I were reluctant to pick up riders. But on this trip we had asked God to use us, so we had to have an open mind about it.

As we approached one young couple, Jean suddenly spoke. "Let's give them a lift."

The bearded young man and the girl with close-cropped hair hadn't been in the car a minute when we realized we were going to have a communication problem. They were Czech, and the girl could speak just a little English, but the boy scarcely any. But as the miles sped by, we slowly and painstakingly elicited something of their story.

The girl's name was Marta Zemanovz, and the boy was Alec Pokorny, though he answered to the name of Ben, a nickname given him by some English students he had met the year before in Prague. They had left home about two weeks before, with the three pounds ($7.20) allowance permitted them by their government. Ben had managed to earn a few pounds cleaning the windows of an English country house, but this and their meager allowance had gone for food and bus fares, and their only food that day had been a bottle of milk for breakfast.

Despite the differences in language and customs, this young couple grew on us. We ate our evening meal together in a Chinese restaurant in Glasgow, took them outside the town so they could camp for the night, gave them a little money for bus fares and food, and then drove off to find somewhere to spend the night ourselves.

Next day we spent the morning with some friends in Glasgow, and on their advice decided to visit the coast resort of Oban by way of Loch Lomond. As we rounded a corner about four miles out of Glasgow, who should be thumbing a lift but Marta and Ben, who had just that minute gotten off a bus.

"Well," said a surprised Jean, "this was meant to be!" We picked them up again and spent the next two days with them. We took them to Fort William, greatly enjoying the Czech folk tunes they sang on the way, and after regretful good-byes left them to make their way home to Czechoslovakia, while we spent the rest of the week on our own.

We hadn't been back home a day or two before the news of the Russian invasion of Czechoslovakia came over the radio. A few days later there came a letter postmarked Germany. "Dear English parents," it began.

"We are in West Germany, but we cannot go to our home because there is the war! Please, help to us! We wish to go back to your free country and work and live there in the time of the war in our country. It is possible to get a room (anywhere) and live there? We are very unhappy of it. It is very terrible for us and for all our people. The foreign soldiers we all hate to have in our homes. Please, can you ask a work and room for us and write the answer very soon to us? We hope it will be possible to go back to your land. What do you mind about it?

"With the hope and love are waiting. Marta and Ben"

"Well," said Jean, "we asked God for a meaning-ful vacation, and He allowed us to share the lives of Marta and Ben, perhaps just so that they might have somewhere to come."

Within ten days, our Czech children had hitch-hiked back across Germany and France, and were in our home. They stayed with us for two weeks, and friends and well-wishers provided them with clothes and supplies. With the help of some Czech people who already lived in England, we found them jobs in a London clothing factory.

To our delight Marta and Ben decided to get mar-ried. Without too much hope that she could get a per-mit, we invited Marta's mother in Czechoslovakia to visit us in England and attend the wedding. She was able to get a permit to come and brought with her for the ceremony a wedding veil that had long been in the family.

At one point before the wedding, the young couple expressed amazement at the series of coincidences that had brought us together. As wisely and lovingly as we could, we told them of our belief in God and the fascinating experiences He brings us when we turn our lives over to Him. "God makes these coincidences happen," we said.

I'm not sure they understood our words, but they read our hearts and knew we cared. And I'm content to leave it there, knowing what miracles God will work in the future through people who let themselves be used by and for Him.

# Perfect Match

*by Mary Smith*

————— ⁓ —————

Christmas was just a few weeks away, and I strolled through the department store, picking up a few items for someone special. Every year I pick a needy child's wish list from the "Angel Tree" at my local mall, hoping to spread a little of the holiday spirit.

Wristwatch, check. A pair of athletic shoes, size six, check. Finally, I grabbed a yellow fleece jacket off the rack and brought everything to the register. It made me feel good picturing that little boy on Christmas Day, his eyes lighting up as he opened his presents. I paid the cashier and decided to take the gifts home to wrap them myself, planning on returning to the mall that night to leave them at the drop-off spot. *Just a few more errands to run first*, I thought.

The day flew by, and I arrived home much later than I expected. I felt absolutely beat. I barely touched my dinner. I went to bed early. The next morning I woke up with a fever. The flu. Oh no. Not now...

It was days before I could resume my Christmas preparations. The Angel Tree! I completely forgot to drop off the gifts! I hopped in the car and sped to the mall, praying that it wasn't too late. But when I got there, the tree was gone. The deadline to drop off gifts had passed. My heart sank. I turned and headed back home. *That poor child won't get anything for Christmas this year and it's all my fault!*

That Sunday I was sitting in church listening to the prayer requests when a woman mentioned a grandmother who was raising her grandson by herself and couldn't afford any gifts for Christmas. *Could this be my chance to make up for what I did?* I thought.

I went up to the woman afterward. "How can I help?" I asked.

"She put her grandson's Christmas wish list on the Angel Tree, but they still haven't received anything," she said.

Right away I perked up. Could it be? "What did he ask for?"

"A wristwatch, a pair of athletic shoes, size six, and a warm jacket, in his favorite color, yellow," she said.

# TUNED IN

*by Sharon L. Markle*

———— ❦ ————

When our church observed "Women in the Pulpit" Sunday, I was asked to give the morning sermon. In college I had enjoyed competing on our debating team, so I was used to speaking in front of people, but talking to my own congregation about faith made me unsure of myself. How could I find a way to convey my convictions?

I chose for my text "the fruit of the Spirit is love, joy, peace, patience, kindness, goodness, faithfulness, gentleness, self-control" (Galatians 5:22–23 NAS). I wanted to show how, when we are close to God, when we truly tune in to Him, we can feel His love working through us and the "fruit of the Spirit" becomes a part of us. In preparation, I prayed earnestly for God's help in finding a simple way to make my point clear.

Then I got an inspiration. I took my twelve-year-old son's small transistor radio with me to the pulpit that Sunday morning. Near the end of my sermon I turned it on and held it up to the microphone. Since I had deliberately set the dial between two stations, loud, fuzzy static blasted through the speakers.

Pulling it away from the mike, I said, "That's what it's like when we're not living close to God. But when we're in tune with Him, we demonstrate love, joy, peace, patience, kindness, goodness, faithfulness, gentleness, and self-control."

At that moment I turned the radio dial to the nearest station to demonstrate the clarity of a properly tuned-in radio. And out came a man's voice intoning words that proved my point better than anything that I myself could possibly have said: "love, joy, peace, patience, kindness, goodness, faithfulness, gentleness, and self-control."

# Miracle in the Census Room

*by Jan Noble*

· · · · · · · · · · · · · · · · · —⁓— · · · · · · · · · · · · · · · · ·

*M*y husband, Rich, who'd been adopted as a baby, always brushed aside questions about whether he'd like to find his birth parents, saying, "If they didn't want me then, it's too late now." Still I knew that his stoic surface hid a deep ache. One night I noticed Rich crying at a TV movie about a father and son. I decided to track down his birth family so he might find some closure.

All I had to go on was the information on Rich's birth certificate: his birthdate, October 16, 1941; his mother's name, Ruth Hicks Casselman; and her place of birth, Waupaca County, Wisconsin. I wrote to the hospital, went through old phone directories, searched the Internet—but no luck.

The only place left to try was the National Archives in Washington, DC. One day I went to check the census records there. But I learned that by law, census information isn't released for seventy-two years. I was crushed. What good was such dated material?

I pulled the latest Waupaca census reel available—1920—from its file drawer. As I passed the first rows of microfilm readers, I overheard a man mention Wisconsin to the older woman with him. *That's interesting*, I thought before going on to my reader.

There was a listing for Hicks—Ruth! Encouraged, I went back for the 1910 reel. Maybe I could get names of relatives to follow up on. The slot where the reel should have been was empty. Then I remembered the folks I had overheard.

I walked over and peeked at their screen. *Ruth Hicks, Waupaca County, 1910!* Amazed, I asked, "May I take a look when you're done? I'm trying to locate the family of Ruth Hicks..."

"...Casselman?" the woman gasped. "She was my mother! Our family split up when I was little and I'm trying to find my baby brother. I've been looking for him for years."

Later that evening over dinner, the last chapter in the family history was finally closed. Shirley Casselman Garnett met her long-lost baby brother, my husband, Rich.

# BEST BIRTHDAY
# PRESENTS EVER

*by Pat Reidelberger*

———————————— ·///· ————————————

All those years my husband, Mel, and I tried and prayed to have children, I'd say on my birthday, "A little girl or little boy would be present enough." And whenever I asked Mel what it was that he wanted for his birthday, he'd always wish for the same.

After doing everything that was medically possible we decided to adopt. For two years we struggled through the process. Finally we were okayed for a private adoption. Our new baby was due to be born at the end of February.

The call came unexpectedly early, on the evening of the sixteenth. We had a son! A healthy baby boy born at four thirty that afternoon. Mel was on his way home from work. As soon as he came in the door I ran to tell him. "What a perfect day for it!" he said, sweeping me off my feet. "Happy birthday!" I had been so excited about our new baby boy, I had almost forgotten what day it was.

Our son, David, and I celebrated birthdays together. "Happy birthday, Mommy and David," our cake would say. And as we blew out the candles together, I knew that my birthday wish had already come true.

We wanted David to have a brother or sister to grow up with, and in time applied to a state agency, Children and Family Services. When David was nine, the social worker brought us a homeless six-year-old girl, dark-haired and wide-eyed.

Sheila arrived at our house on a Friday night and we were supposed to keep her just for the weekend to see how she adjusted to life with our family. But by Saturday night she was insisting that she wasn't going anywhere. "I want to stay right here," she said. Sheila had adopted us.

Only when doing the paperwork to finalize the adoption did I happen to notice something amazing.

"Look," I said to Mel, pointing to the line on the document carrying Sheila's birth date. "She was born on July 18. Your birthday!"

A little girl and little boy. The best presents a parent could ever have.

# LEMON CHEESECAKE

*by Peggy Piland*

————— ⁂ —————

*I* had planned to make brown-sugar pound cake, my specialty, for my Sunday school teacher, Mrs. Howell, who had been in my thoughts. But suddenly the idea to bake her a cheesecake popped into mind—a lemon cheesecake.

The recipe called for fresh lemons. I checked my supplies. No lemons, but plenty of brown sugar. A pound cake would be so much easier, I thought.

But again came the nudge: *Bake a lemon cheesecake.* After a trip to the grocery for lemons, I began the batter. I cut a lemon in half, removed the seeds, squeezed the juice into the creamy mixture, and stirred.

When I arrived at Mrs. Howell's, her husband let me in. "She'll be happy to see you," he said. Then he explained Mrs. Howell had broken her leg and was bedridden. "The doctor says she'll be fine. But she's frustrated because she can't get around like she's used to."

I walked into the bedroom, carrying my surprise. "I'm so sorry about your leg, Mrs. Howell," I said. "Maybe this will make you feel better." As I placed the cake on a table, the tangy scent of fresh lemons wafted through the air. I looked at Mrs. Howell. She was crying.

"How did you know?" she asked.

"Know?"

"Today is our wedding anniversary," she said. "For the past fifty-three years I've baked my husband his favorite thing." She pointed at the cake. "How did you know it was lemon cheesecake?"

# THE MYSTERIOUS
# RED SLED

*by Dave Mahler*

...................... —ɯ— ......................

Zach, our twelve-year-old, woke up the day after Thanksgiving and let out a loud *whoop*. It had snowed. Not just a dusting either, but a thick blanket. He bugged his older brothers, Jake and Mike, until they finally agreed to take him sledding.

Later that afternoon the phone rang. It was Mike. His voice was tense. "Dad, you need to get here right away. Jake's hurt. He can't talk. He can't move. Hurry!"

But Mike didn't know where they were. Jake had driven and Mike hadn't paid much attention to where they went. The only landmark he could remember was the Groveland Elementary School. I called 911, told them to send an ambulance to the school parking lot, then drove there with my wife, Marilee. The police and EMTs showed up minutes after we did. I explained the situation. We racked our brains. Nobody could think of any sledding hills in the area.

I called Mike. "I can't see the main road," he said, "just a lot of houses. But I definitely heard sirens."

We were close. "We'll drive around. If you hear the sirens again, try to follow the sound and flag us down."

With police car and ambulance right behind me, sirens blaring, I drove a few blocks until Marilee said she saw a boy at the side of the road. He had a red sled in one hand and was waving at us with the other. Zach. *Thank God,* I thought. I turned left. Zach had vanished. I drove on. No Zach. No tracks, even. Then I saw it—Mike's car. I stopped, got out, and saw our sons at the bottom of a hill, Jake lying on the ground. The EMTs rushed him to the hospital. His injuries were severe. He was hospitalized for weeks. But by New Year's Eve he was well on the way to recovery. That night we sat in his room and talked about what had happened. "Zach, I'm so glad you flagged us down," Marilee said.

"I what?" he asked. "Mike and I stayed with Jake till you got there."

"I saw you," Marilee said. "I couldn't have missed that red sled of yours."

"But Mom," Zach said, "I don't have a red sled."

# THE BEST NURSING CARE

*by Annette Perdue*

· · · · · · · · · · · · · · · · · · · · ·  ·  —〰〰—  ·  · · · · · · · · · · · · · · · · · · · · ·

We needed to find a nurse to help care for my mother, Mary Pittman. And not just any nurse. Mother had been a registered nurse herself. The world's best, people said. She worked for Dr. Zdanis until she was almost eighty years old. She practically ran that office. She was the best caregiver I'd ever known. She could soothe a crying child or calm a worried parent. Everyone felt better after she was done with them. And that was even before they saw the doctor.

But then she got Parkinson's disease and had to retire. Now she was the one who needed to be taken care of. My brother, Pat, moved in with her. They had a few good years together. But Mother got so bad we had to put her into a nursing home.

The facility we chose had an excellent reputation. The staff treated Mother with great compassion. Still, she wasn't happy there. She never told us so, but it was obvious. All she wanted was to go back to her own home. That's what my brother thought would be best too.

So we made arrangements with the hospice people and took Mother back home. Pat and I worried about who they would send to care for her. Not that she would ever complain, mind you. But the best nurse in the world certainly deserved the best nursing care in her final days, and that's what my brother and I hoped and prayed for: a nurse who would care for Mother the way she had cared for others.

The first day a beautiful young woman with a big, confident smile showed up. The first thing she asked Mother was, "Didn't you used to work for Dr. Zdanis?"

"I certainly did," Mother said. "Until I was almost eighty." Even in her weakened state you could still hear the pride in her voice.

"I recognized the name in your file," she said. "And now that I'm here, there's no doubt. You see, when I was a little girl, you took care of me. I always loved and admired you," she told Mother, taking her hand. "In fact, you're one of the main reasons I became a nurse."

# GIVE AND *IT* SHALL BE GIVEN TO YOU

*by Mary Jarvis*

---

*I* lifted the heavy lid of our old freezer in the garage and peered inside, looking for some vegetables to make for dinner. For the past year, we'd scraped by on my small teacher's salary while my husband, Mike, was away at graduate school. With three hungry teenagers to feed, it was a challenge to stretch our grocery dollars. Now, one glance at the half-empty freezer made me question what I'd done on impulse a week earlier.

The Tuesday before Thanksgiving, Kathy, my fourteen-year-old, blurted out that one of her friends wasn't celebrating the holiday because her mother couldn't afford it. "We could give them our turkey, Mom," she said. "We don't need it since we're going to Uncle Pat's." How could I explain to her that I was saving our turkey for Christmas? We didn't have enough money for Mike to come home for Thanksgiving. The kids and I were going to my brother-in-law's so I wouldn't have to invest in a big dinner. How could I afford another turkey before Christmas?

We taught our kids to help others. But to help someone else when we could barely help ourselves? Still, I knew I couldn't say no. *Lord, I hope You have a plan because I sure don't.*

We gathered up a bag of potatoes and cranberry sauce I had in the pantry. I sent my son, Matt, out to the freezer in the garage to get some vegetables— and the turkey. When we brought Kathy's friend the food, her mother cried tears of joy. At the time, their happiness made me feel better about giving away our turkey. But now, looking into our freezer, I wondered, *Who's going to help us?*

I rummaged through the frozen containers— broccoli, carrots, some blackberries from our garden. I pushed aside some frosted bags of green beans and corn. Wait...something was there. Suddenly I stopped and stared. Nestled among the vegetables was a newly bought turkey.

I never found out who the mysterious donor was. Does it matter? Whoever it was knew exactly what we needed, when we needed it.

# 2
# EXTRAORDINARY PROTECTION

For he will command his angels concerning you to guard you in all your ways; they will lift you up in their hands, so that you will not strike your foot against a stone.

PSALM 91:11–12 NIV

———⁓⁓———

*Gracious heavenly Father, what a comfort it is to know that we are safe in Your hands.*

# THE STURDY BLUE SPRUCE

*by James Haney*

............................ ⸺〰⸺ ............................

$M$any years ago, during one of our visits to see family in Silver Lake, Indiana, I decided to give my parents a tree for their yard. My wife, Marilyn, and I took our four young sons to a nursery and we picked out a sturdy blue spruce sapling.

"Someday," I told the boys as we planted the tree, "this will be big enough to protect Grandma and Grandpa's house from the sun and wind." Over the years it was a pleasure to see how tall and beautiful the spruce was growing.

Eventually my parents passed away, but we still went to Silver Lake to visit the rest of the family. I took up flying, and once the boys were grown Marilyn and I made the 1,400-mile journey from our home in Idaho in my single-engine Piper PA-16.

One October it was again time for a visit. We circled the Silver Lake area to signal Marilyn's sister and her husband to pick us up at the airport.

Without warning, our engine quit. We went into a steep dive. As the earth rushed toward us, I realized we were headed straight for my childhood home!

Praying desperately that no one would be hurt, I braced for the inevitable impact. But, instead of smashing into the house, something soft cushioned our breakneck fall. We skidded to a halt in the yard across the street.

Later, one of the rescue workers who helped us out of the wreckage told us, "It's amazing you didn't hit the house or power lines. That big blue spruce probably saved your lives." A long-ago gift to my parents had ended up protecting my wife and me.

# Not a Scratch

*by Margie Miyoshi*

---

*I*t was the afternoon of the annual sukiyaki dinner, my church's biggest fund-raiser of the year, where our predominantly Japanese-American congregation invites the community to share a meal. I was chair of the event and I had been busy all day getting food ready and organizing the other volunteers. Two of the people helping out had to leave, so I took them home. Driving back to the church along the four-lane highway, I was completely exhausted.

I felt my eyelids growing heavy. *Just a little bit farther*, I thought. *I'm almost there*. I turned up the radio and turned on the air. But the headlights blurred in front of me. Everything moved in slow motion.

The next thing I knew, there was a loud screeching sound, a heavy grinding from underneath the car, sparks flying. The car had run into the median separating the lanes of traffic. Instinctively, I gripped the steering wheel and steadied the car, my eyes open wide.

*Thank God for that median*, I thought, shaking. I could have crossed into the other lanes and right into an oncoming car!

When I got back to the church I told everyone what had happened.

"Was there a lot of damage?" Joe, a fellow volunteer, asked.

"I was afraid to look," I told him. We went back to the parking lot to check out my car.

*What if it's serious?* I thought. I braced myself for the worst. But to my surprise, there wasn't any damage to be seen. No scrapes on the frame, not a dent on the tire rim, not even a scratch. Joe and I looked underneath and around the car, but couldn't find anything wrong.

*It's a miracle*, I thought.

A few weeks later I was driving down the same stretch of road where I'd had my accident. Maybe there's still some tire rubber on the median, I thought. I kept glancing over along the middle of the road, curious to see where my car had hit.

I kept looking. But never saw it. There was no median to be found. Not even a sign of one.

# Saved by a Phone Call

*by Keith Pulles*

———ɯ———

I t's time to shock the pool and shut it down for winter," Dad said that September day. He was right. You could feel the nip of fall in the air. But at nine, closing the pool meant summer was definitely over. I wasn't sure what "shocking" meant. "All it means is using special strong chemicals to clean up the water," Dad explained. "That way the pool will stay in good shape even though it's covered all winter long."

Dad went out to the yard and I watched glum-ly from the window as he opened a jug and started dumping stuff into the pool. Then he got another jug. More stuff. *That's a lot of stuff to put into the pool,* I thought. Just then the phone rang. I ran to check the caller ID. "Unknown name, unknown number," flashed back at me. Normally I only picked up the phone when I saw it was someone I knew. Mom and Dad had warned me about talking to strangers. But that day a voice inside said, *Pick it up!* The urge was so strong and insistent, I lifted the receiver to my ear. "Hello?"

"May I speak with Steve Pulles, please?" I didn't recognize the voice. A telemarketer, probably. They were always calling. Dad wouldn't want whatever it was this guy was trying to sell. But again, something made me open my mouth and say, "Hang on. I'll go get him."

I went outside, through the garage door, phone in hand. "Dad! Phone!"

"Who's calling?" he hollered to me.

"Dunno."

Dad walked around the side of the garage from the backyard and took the cordless from me. "Hello? Hello...?" A couple of seconds later he took the phone from his ear and turned it off. "Nobody there," he said.

Suddenly there was an enormous *boom* from out back. "The pool!" Dad shouted. Turned out he'd mixed together two chemicals he shouldn't have. The mixture exploded out of the water, leaving toxic fumes. The fumes dissipated, but... "If I'd been out here," Dad said later, "I could have died."

Unknown caller? I don't think so. The person on the phone that day certainly had our number.

# NEARLY FATAL

*by Wilda Lahmann*

———— ※ ————

$\mathcal{M}$y husband, Randy, shook me awake. It must have been 2:00 AM. He was hunched over, holding a hand to his chest. "Wilda, I need to get to the hospital," he said, gasping. "Can't breathe."

"I'll call 911," I said, jumping out of bed.

"No time," he gasped again. "Drive me. Now."

I helped him up and got him out to our van. Randy slumped against the passenger-side door. Fifteen miles to the hospital. *Too far,* I thought. *We're not going to make it. Send help, Lord.*

We tore out of the driveway, engine roaring in the still night air. Could Randy hold on? About a mile down the road, at the bottom of a hill, I saw something in the street. Were my eyes playing tricks on me? No, it was real. An ambulance!

"Look, Randy!" I shouted. A paramedic stood outside the vehicle. Was he waiting for us? Who could have known to call?

I slammed on the brakes, leaped out of the van, and ran over to the ambulance, screaming for help. The paramedic and his partner went right to work. "Possible cardiac," one said. They strapped an oxygen mask onto Randy and started treatment. Then they loaded him onto a stretcher and into the ambulance, unconscious. "Follow us," one of them told me.

The next three days were touch-and-go. I never left Randy's bedside, praying he'd wake up. Finally, he did. "What happened?" he asked.

"You mean you don't remember?"

"Nothing after the ambulance," he said.

"You had a massive heart attack. The EMTs said another minute or two and..." I squeezed his hand tight.

"You called them?" Randy asked.

"No," I told him. "They received a report of a car crash at that intersection. They even called in to make sure that they were at the right location. They were. And then we came along seconds later."

Fifteen miles on empty roads in the middle of the night. Randy's heart attack would have been fatal if those paramedics hadn't been there. I'd say they were in the perfect location.

# CONFUSED AND FAR FROM HOME

*by Rebecca Yauger*

---

The doorbell rang just as I was about to go to bed. Strange. I peered out the window. What was an elderly woman doing on my porch at that time of night? She seemed upset. Her hair and clothes were disheveled. I opened the door.

"Can I help you?" I asked. The woman stepped right into the foyer as if she knew where she was going. Then she stopped and looked around, a confused expression on her face. "Where's Al?" she asked. "I want you to call Al."

"Who's Al?" I asked her. She stared at me and didn't answer, so I repeated the question.

"My son-in-law," the woman said. "Al's my son-in-law. I want you to call him." Her voice wavered. She sounded like she was on the verge of panic.

I tried to get her to sit down, but she only became more agitated. I brought her a glass of water. That didn't help, either. She just repeated the same thing over and over again. "Call Al. I want you to call Al."

"What's Al's last name?" I asked. She looked at me blankly. Suddenly she said, "Sanders. Al Sanders."

"Al Sanders? I know that name!" I said. "I work with an Al Sanders." I ran to my desk where I kept the company directory. I pulled it out, looked up Al's number, and dialed.

"It's Becky from work," I said when he picked up. "I know this sounds crazy, but there's a woman at my house who says that she's your mother-in-law and . . ."

"Thank God!" Al exclaimed. "You're an answer to prayer, Becky. I'll be right over. Please tell her I'm on my way."

Al's mother-in-law was as happy to see him as he was to see her. Al explained that she had Alzheimer's and had wandered away from her nursing home. This wasn't the first time, either.

"She's never gone this far, though," he said. "The nursing home is almost three miles away from here. She had to cross the main boulevard. But it's a miracle that out of all these houses she came to yours. Who else would have had my number? It's unlisted."

# SAVED BY AN OPEN DOOR

*by Sheri Bull*

————— ✦ —————

*H*ere in the Midwest, we're used to frigid winters, but that morning seemed colder than usual. Maybe it was because my husband wasn't sleeping next to me. He had gone out of town on a long trip. It was just me looking after our three daughters. We lived out in the country—no neighbors within shouting distance, and I felt vulnerable. At night I made sure to lock the doors and I prayed God would watch over us.

I'd woken up shivering, with a pounding headache. It was really cold, even for our 170-year-old house. Did our furnace break down? I went downstairs to check. That's when I saw that the front door was wide open! I shut it and cranked up the thermostat. *I'm positive I locked that door last night. Did someone break in?* I dashed upstairs. The girls were safe in their beds. I looked around. Nothing was missing.

My teeth chattering, I waited for the furnace to kick in. It didn't. The draft from the door must have blown the pilot light out. I didn't know how to relight it. My husband usually took care of things like that. Why did he have to be gone for so long?

I called the girls down to breakfast, turning on the oven and shoving the kitchen table near it for warmth.

Once I got the kids off to school and I got to work, I phoned a furnace repairman. "I'll take a look as soon as I can and call you," he said.

I got a call back a few hours later. "Your furnace has a leak," the repairman said, in a tone that seemed to imply more than just a minor problem.

"How soon can you fix it?" I asked, dreading another freezing night.

"Ma'am, you don't understand," he said. "Your furnace is leaking carbon monoxide. That's the type of thing you see on the news, where an entire family dies in their sleep. I'll install a new furnace tomorrow. Until then, you'll need to stay somewhere else."

Immediately I thought of the front door. If it hadn't somehow gotten open to let the fresh air in . . .

That breath of fresh air saved our lives—and it made an impression on my husband too. When he got home, he promised never to leave us for so long again.

# MYSTERY MENU

*by Imogene Wagster*

················ —ᴡᴡ— ················

One day after eating shrimp salad I itched everywhere, my lips swelled, and my throat began to close. "You're allergic to the iodine in shrimp," my family doctor said. "Don't eat it again."

Several years later I was admitted to the hospital for surgery. *God, I'm so nervous. Please be with me.* Among the forms I was given to complete was the menu for dinner, and shrimp was one of the choices. Of course I crossed it off and chose another entrée. Later the anesthesiologist asked if I was allergic to any medications. "I'm allergic to shrimp," I said. Ordinarily I wouldn't have thought to mention foods, but because of the menu, it was on my mind. The anesthesiologist scrawled something on my chart and left.

That afternoon I was wheeled off and given a purple dye to drink for a test. But a nurse suddenly appeared and stopped me. "Your test has been canceled," she said.

My surgery proceeded and I awoke to hear that everything went well. "But it's a good thing you told us about your shrimp allergy and we canceled that test," my doctor said. "There's iodine in the purple dye and the consequences could have been disastrous."

When the dietitian came to discuss my meals that evening I told her how thankful I was that shrimp had been on the hospital menu the day before.

She looked at me strangely. "That couldn't have been," she said. "We never serve shrimp to our patients."

# BLIND AND LOST

## by Thelma Leavy

—⁂—

*I* have always loved the snow. I'm eighty-five and le-
gally blind, but I can see light and some shapes—and I
still get excited by fluffy flakes. That's why I ventured
out late one snowy afternoon last winter.

I shuffled down my long driveway to my favorite
Douglas fir. I went from tree to tree, shaking snow
from the boughs. Soon I noticed that I was surrounded
by vague unfamiliar shapes. I'd gone too far into the
woods! I turned and started walking back toward my
driveway. But which way had I come? Everything was
so white. And cold. The snow fell harder. Wiping
tears from my eyes, I rushed forward in a panic.
"God," I cried, "please help me."

Abruptly I stopped in my tracks.

I stood perfectly still as a feeling of relief broke
through my fear. Then I turned completely around
and struck out in a new direction. Finally I came to a

fence. It was my boundary line! I followed that fence, just hung to it, until I reached my gate. "Thank You, God," I said.

The next morning, Dan, the young man who shovels snow for me, came rushing in, alarmed by the footsteps he had seen on the snow-covered property. "Don't worry," I quickly explained, "they're mine."

"Mrs. Leavy," Dan said, "I followed those footsteps. They lead up to the edge of the riverbank, right to where the drop-off is steepest. If you'd taken even one more step forward . . ."

But that was where I had stopped and called out— to the One who always leads in the right direction.

# WHEN *I* HEEDED
## A NUDGE

*by Mary Jane Hicks*

————— ⁓ —————

*I*'d been selling cosmetics and delivering orders to
people in their homes all day and I was tired and
achy. Just out of bed from an attack of flu, I knew I
should hurry home. But a few blocks from our street,
I stopped. I thought of another customer, Nellie May
White, a sweet, retired schoolteacher I'd known all
my life. *Go see her*, something seemed to say to me.

I tapped at Nellie May's door. No answer.

I knocked again. Usually, I only had to rap once.
No answer. I wanted to turn and leave, but my feet
seemed glued to that porch.

I knocked a third time, and now, at last, Nellie
May opened the door and invited me in. I gave her
the cosmetics she'd ordered and she paid me. How
pale she seemed. How unsteady on her feet she was.

"Come into the kitchen, my dear," she said, and as I followed her down the hall, I thought there was something strange about the air I was breathing.

"Now," she said, taking out a checkbook, "how much do I owe you?"

"Nellie May, you just paid me!" Then, without wasting another second, I sniffed the air and followed the faint, acrid odor into the dining room. The gas log in the fireplace there was turned on, and the flame had gone out. I could smell lethal fumes seeping from it.

We got out fast. I took Nellie May to a doctor, who immediately hospitalized her.

"I don't know how you happened along just when you did," she said later.

I do.

# Right Place at the Right Time

*by Mary Jane Kelsch*

My husband, Walt, and I live just down the street from the rectory, so when Father Nuwer caught pneumonia that March we offered to help in any way we could. We'd be happy to bring him a hot meal, take him to a doctor's appointment—whatever he needed. Walt and I were both retired, so we had plenty of free time.

"Don't hesitate to call on us day or night," Walt told Father Nuwer. "We are always here for you."

We were cleaning up after dinner one evening when the phone rang. It was Father Nuwer.

"I'm having trouble breathing," he said, his voice raspy and strained. "Can you drive me to the hospital?"

"I'll be right over," Walt said. He threw on his coat and shoes and dashed out the door.

Walt got into our car and headed for the rectory. I tried to watch some TV, but I couldn't concentrate on anything; I was too worried. Father Nuwer was asthmatic. I knew that if he had a serious asthma attack on top of his pneumonia, it could kill him.

I stared at the clock, trying to guess when they'd reach the emergency room and how long it would take to see a doctor. Minutes ticked by, then hours. It was nearly 11:00 PM. *Why hasn't Walt called?* I wondered. *Is Father Nuwer going to be okay?*

Just as I was about to shut off the TV, the phone rang. I grabbed the receiver.

"Walt?"

But it was my daughter, Donna.

"Don't worry, Mom," she told me. "The hospital just let me know that he's all right."

"Thank goodness," I said. "But why would the hospital call you about Father Nuwer?"

"Father Nuwer?" Donna asked. "He's fine. He must have had the hospital call me first. It's Dad. He had a heart attack. The doctor said that if they hadn't been able to use the defibrillator on him right away, he might not have made it."

Donna paused. "Lucky thing Dad was right there in the emergency room when it happened."

Lucky? I think it was more than that.

# A BEACON IN THE STORM

*by Mary G. Beasley*

———— ⁓ ————

Rain pelted my Volkswagen Beetle. I put the wipers on high and peered through the windshield. Storm clouds hovered above Highway 301 as far as I could see, blotting out the sunset. Lightning blazed across the horizon and thunder rumbled ominously from the northwest. Forget making it all the way to North Carolina. I needed a place to stay for the night before the wind blew me off the road.

But where? I was right smack in the middle of the Georgia swamplands. There was nothing for miles. No motels, not even a gas station or a convenience store where I could stop and ask someone for directions.

Normally I didn't mind driving alone, but now I was worried. I was heading straight into the path of the storm. And, boy, it sure looked to be a nasty one. I had to get off the highway quickly.

The rain was really coming down now. *Wait, what's that?* I squinted. There it was: a brightly lit sign. MRS. SMITH'S INN.

I pulled off the highway and stopped in front of a gracious Southern home. Wraparound porch, wicker rocking chairs, and all. The porch swing swayed violently in the wind.

I ducked my head and dashed up the steps. At the door an older woman greeted me with a sweet, motherly smile. "How can I help you, dear?"

"Do you happen to have a room for the night?" I asked.

"I'm so sorry, we're all filled up," she said. "There's a convention in town, and we have been booked solid for weeks. I'm afraid every room in town is taken."

Dejected, I slowly turned to go. Another clap of thunder.

"Wait," she said. "I'll set up my hideaway bed in the kitchen. You can have my room."

I breathed a prayer of thanks and signed the register.

"Out of curiosity," the woman asked, "why did you decide to stop here?"

"Well, I saw your sign from the highway. It had such a welcoming glow."

"My sign?" she said. "Why, that old thing hasn't worked for ages."

# Out of Sight

*by Dixie Borneman*

--- ∿ ---

Kept busy with all the jobs that a housewife has, plus helping handicapped children learn to swim, I hadn't done any sewing for months. But for some reason, on this particular morning I decided to spend a few extra minutes at my sewing machine upstairs.

I was in the middle of a seam when the sound of honking horns from the highway in front of our house made me glance out the window. At first I saw only the choppy waters of Greenlake beyond the highway. It was February, and angry wind was blowing from across the lake, shaking the trees that dotted the shore.

Then I saw a boy about five years old, alone, crossing the busy highway. I had never seen a child so bundled up in winter clothing. I watched as he made it safely through the traffic and headed toward the shore of the lake. Even though dozens of cars were on the highway, and the lake was rimmed with houses, a curious realization came to me: *You are the only one who knows that boy is out there. Hurry!*

I raced downstairs, but since the shore of the lake isn't visible from the main floor of our house, I lost sight of the boy as I hurried toward the door. I grabbed a light sweater, thinking it would take a few minutes to bring him back to safety. For some strange reason, despite the weather, I didn't stop to put on my coat.

I got halfway across the highway, but the cars were coming too fast to cross the other half. I stood impatiently on the median and scanned the shore. The child had vanished. Then in one fantastic second my eye glimpsed a hand sticking up from the murky water, about twelve feet from shore. In an instant the hand disappeared.

The traffic broke, and I began to run, my eyes hardly leaving the spot where I'd seen the hand. My years of swimming had prepared me for this moment, and I knew how vital each second had now become. I can't remember removing my sweater and shoes, I don't remember jumping the five-foot bank that led to the shore, I didn't see the rugged boulders or broken bottles that I must have landed near. With my eyes still on the spot, I neither dived nor swam but hopscotched through the water. If I didn't locate the youngster immediately, it would be too late.

Suddenly I spotted him on the bottom of the lake; his brown-green jacket had already blended with the brown-green of the silt. I never would have found him if I had taken my eyes off the spot where I'd seen his hand. I reached down into the cold water, grabbed his jacket, and pulled him up. Then I hoisted his body onto mine, brought him to the surface, and headed for shore.

As I reached shore, an elderly fisherman suddenly appeared and extended his hand to help me. Even in that desperate moment I marveled at the coincidence that the old man should be there. Pulling up on a bulkhead, I put the child on his back and began re-suscitation. At last, his breath began to return.

Not until then was I aware of the near-freezing cold and the violent wind. The boy was alive, yet the cold could still kill him. He had been so bundled against the weather that now, out of the water, his thick boots and soaked garments made him a dead weight, and I found it impossible, even with the help of the old fisherman, to lift him.

Then I looked up into the face of Dennis Losse, a man whom I had often seen jogging around the lake alone. Without being asked, he lifted the boy. I motioned toward my house, and we began hurrying to it. He told me that for years he had jogged around the lake once a day, but on a strange impulse had decided today to circle it twice. From the distance he had seen my racing flight and had come to save me from what looked like an attempt at suicide.

In my kitchen we peeled off the boy's wet clothing. Although cold and shivering, he seemed all right. I called the police, then went to change my clothes. In a few minutes the police arrived with the child's mother. She was beside herself with joy over her son's safe return.

Finally I was alone. I walked back up to the sewing room and looked out the window. The coincidences of the past hour raced through my mind, and I marveled how each event had connected so perfectly. Suddenly I was sure that these had not been coincidences. The whole rescue had been part of a perfect plan—God's plan. Each person had been uniquely prepared and obedient for his role in it.

As my eyes turned again to the gray water of Greenlake, my mind grasped a new thought. Perhaps all our lives are parts of God's plan. If so, we should live them for helping others in any way we can.

# STUCK IN THE MEXICAN JUNGLE

*by John Tucker*

———— ✹ ————

*I*'d never known the darkness could be so enveloping. The thick Mexican jungle loomed all around us as my wife, Trudy, and I drove toward Villahermosa, where we'd be staying the night. It was the nearest town, and we'd foolishly thought we could reach it by nightfall, but the sun had long since set and the road was slow going. I concentrated on the short beam of our headlights as we moved through the moonless night.

"Well, we wanted to be someplace remote, didn't we?" I said, trying not to sound worried. Trudy and I had long yearned to serve as missionaries in a faraway locale. When we heard about the desperate needs in the most desolate parts of Mexico, we packed our car and set off down the Pan-American Highway.

But now my imagination was working overtime as I peered at the shadows along the roadside. Suddenly our headlights flickered. I tightened my grip on the steering wheel, squinting out the windshield. *God, we came here to do Your work, and we're trusting You to watch over us,* I prayed.

A few miles farther the lights flickered again, then died. I turned the switch off and on. Nothing. I cut the engine, and we sat in stunned silence. We hadn't seen another car for hours and there was no way to call for help. Walking anywhere in the pitch blackness was out of the question.

"I think we'd better spend the night in the car," I told Trudy. We pulled a blanket over the two of us and went to sleep. Next thing I knew, Trudy was shaking me awake. "John, look!" she exclaimed. My eyes adjusted to the sunlight and I saw what Trudy was pointing at. Directly ahead of us the road narrowed and then abruptly ended.

We got out of the car and walked to the road's edge. A swift river ran below. Building materials for a bridge were stacked on the bank. "We never would have had time to stop," Trudy said.

After we made it to town I pulled over to try to fix the lights. But they worked fine. And they never flickered once the rest of the trip.

# LOOKING OUT FOR GRANDMA

*by Dave Kenshol*

.................... —⟩⟨⟨— ....................

*I* used to travel a lot when I was a regional manager for Sears. Once I had a last-minute meeting at our corporate headquarters in Chicago. While weaving my way through the bustling Sky Harbor Airport in Phoenix, I thought of all the things that could mess up the trip—delayed departure, bad weather, broken equipment. That got me thinking about the flight my grandmother, Maude Staunifer, would soon be taking. Grandma had been living with my uncle Ray for several years here in Arizona, but now, at ninety-eight, her health was failing. We'd decided to move her into a nursing home that was close to three of her sons and their children and grandchildren, instead of being near just Ray and me in Arizona.

Knowing how happy Grandma would be surrounded by family, I was certain it was the best thing to do. The only thing worrying me was Grandma's flight to Chicago. Both Ray and I worked long hours at our jobs, and Grandma, never wanting to inconvenience anyone, refused to allow either of us to take time off to accompany her. "I can handle it," she had assured us.

Reluctantly we agreed. But now that I was at the airport myself, I was having second thoughts. Had we made a mistake in giving in? So much could go wrong, and I wasn't sure Grandma would be able to manage alone, despite her protestations to the contrary. *God, maybe You can find someone to help look after her,* I prayed.

Since I'd left the final details to Ray, I didn't even know when Grandma's flight was. *I'll call Ray after I land,* I told myself, trying to push my worries out of my mind as I made my way to the gate. At the check-in counter two people were in line ahead of me. I overheard the man trying to arrange seating for an older woman in a wheelchair. She was going to be on my flight to Chicago.

I reached out and took the handles of the wheelchair from the man, telling him, "Ray, why doesn't Grandma sit next to me?"

# Attacked by Bees

### by Pearl Maurer

———⁓———

*I* was gardening one afternoon at our summer cottage on Lake Ontario. I'd grabbed a clump of weeds near an old tree trunk when I suddenly recoiled. Too late. Out swarmed a squad of angry bees. I got a nasty sting on my hand—I had forgotten my gloves.

I yanked out the stinger and rushed toward the cottage for ice, but I didn't get far. Nausea and dizziness swept over me, then I had trouble breathing. *I'm having a reaction. I've got to get help.* My husband was working and the kids were in town with their friends. I glanced across the yard to see if my neighbor Donna was around. No car in the driveway, no sign of anyone home.

My whole arm was swelling now and my joints ached. Only a rising sense of panic kept me moving. *Maybe Donna's parents are home.* Their cottage was right behind Donna's. I staggered out of the yard, past two driveways. *I'm not going to make it.* I tried to shout. No words came out. I made it to the porch steps, praying, *Somebody be home. Please hear me!*

The last thing I remember was reaching for the doorbell.

When I came to, people were hovering around me. "She's DOA," one said. *No, I'm not!* I thought before slipping back into unconsciousness.

I awoke in a hospital bed with a doctor standing over me. He looked relieved. I glanced around the room. There were Donna, my husband, and the kids. "Good thing you got here when you did, Mrs. Maurer," the doctor said. "Another few minutes and you wouldn't have survived that allergic reaction to the bee sting. You went into anaphylactic shock."

The doctors kept me overnight for observation. In the morning, Donna came by to fill in the gaps in my memory. "You rang my parents' bell and then collapsed. They told me they heard the bell and came running."

"Thank God they did!"

"That's the odd part. They're both almost completely deaf. They haven't been able to hear that doorbell in years."

# A Way of Escape

### by Dennis Hayzlett

*D*riving through an icy rainstorm, we were headed to a mountain resort for the weekend. Wipers slashing, shoulders tense, I focused on the winding six-lane highway ahead. A dozen cars zipped passed us, but I held my speed down. With my wife, Kathy, and thirteen-year-old son, Jeff, in the car, I didn't want to take any chances.

As I approached a sweeping right-hand curve, the car suddenly skidded. We spun across the highway hurtling straight for the steel guardrail. I glimpsed the fear in Kathy's and Jeff's faces. I said a prayer and braced for the crash.

It never came. The car came to a screeching halt. Now we were turned completely around and stood directly in the path of oncoming traffic. A bank of blinding headlights raced toward us. *I've got to get out of their way!*

I saw an off-ramp behind me. I shoved the gear-shift into Reverse and backed onto the ramp just as the cars whizzed by on the highway. *That was a close one,* I thought.

At the bottom of the off-ramp we came upon a quaint whitewashed general store with a wide front porch and stenciled lettering on the windows. An antique lamppost and old-fashioned gas pumps stood outside.

"Everybody okay?" I asked, looking around. My wife squeezed my hand and Jeff nodded.

We sat for a while in the soft glow of the lamplight. No one seemed to be around but the atmosphere itself calmed us completely.

After a few minutes, when our nerves were settled, we drove back to the highway and continued our trip.

A few days later on the way home we took the same highway. Thinking we'd stop for a bite to eat, we looked for the off-ramp and little store. But they weren't there. Since that weekend, we've traveled the same stretch of highway scores of times and never found that off-ramp or store again. But when we had needed them, they were there.

# Don't Put Your Hands in the Water!

*by Cherie Herrera*

---

Living in Fiji, I couldn't argue with the superlatives used to describe the South Pacific jewel where my parents were missionaries. What seventeen-year-old wouldn't be awed by the beauty of the crystal-clear water, the lushness of the palm trees and sugarcane fields, the fragrance of the soft tropical breezes?

Then came the beginning of the long wet season in November. The daily soaking rains wore on my nerves. Worse, though, was the violence of the tropical gales that could strike the islands at any time. The sound of the rain pounding on the tin roof was deafening and our wooden house shuddered.

One afternoon, about three o'clock, lightning flashed and thunder crashed. Still, I kept washing the lunch dishes.

I was determined not to let the storm get to me. Then something unexplainable came over me. *Stop. Get away.* I had to step back from the sink.

Just then there was a thunderclap so loud it drowned out my terrified scream. All the lightbulbs in the house exploded and the microwave blew up. The air reeked of acrid smoke.

The storm over, Dad went outside to inspect the house. The roof was fine, but our water tank was damaged. Lightning had hit it, sending electric current through our pipes and wires. I remembered my fear and how I had stepped suddenly away from the sink.

The very next day my grandmother phoned me from back home in Cincinnati. "Are you all okay?" she asked. "My friend Donna called. She was upset. She woke up at ten o'clock at night with a terrible sense that you were in danger. She had an overwhelming urge to pray for you."

Ten? That would've been around three in the afternoon in Fiji, right after lunch, when the storm hit. Just before Grandma hung up, she said, "Oh, there's one more thing. Donna prayed specifically. Over and over she felt compelled to pray, 'Don't put your hands in the water.'"

Half a world away, I had gotten the warning.

# Mayday!

*by Hilary Hemingway*

My father was a commercial fisherman when I was young and he had to spend long weeks at sea. One day shortly after I'd turned ten, he was scheduled to be off the coast of Jamaica. We were at our home in Miami. Mom was washing the dinner dishes when her face drained of color. "Mayday," she whispered.

Without even wiping her hands, Mom grabbed the phone. She called the Coast Guard and told the man on duty that she was concerned about her husband.

"Yes, ma'am, we know your husband sure did run into some trouble," he replied. "They're having a heavy storm and he radioed in for help when his boat started taking in water. We flew out there about an hour ago and dropped him a heavy-duty bilge pump."

"I don't believe that the pump is working," Mom insisted. "You need to do another flyover."

The man tried to placate Mom. "He must be all right, Mrs. Hemingway, or we would've heard from him."

"You haven't gotten a Mayday?"

"No, but we'll let you know if we hear anything." Mom hung up. Without saying a word, she went into her bedroom and knelt by her bed. An hour passed. Mom came out, looking even more anxious. She called the Coast Guard again. This time she had steel in her voice. "You had better send a plane out right now or you'll be retrieving the bodies of Leicester Hemingway and his crew."

They said they would send out a rescue plane as soon as possible.

Mom was awake that whole night praying. Early in the morning the phone rang. It was the Coast Guard. They had found my father and his crew floating in debris fifteen miles off Jamaica. Dad's boat had sunk, but all were safe.

Dad arrived home that same afternoon, weary and sunburnt. "The bilge pump they dropped didn't work fast enough," he said. "Too much water was coming in. It started pouring over our transom. I radioed in a Mayday, but my call never got through."

But it had—to Mom.

# REVEALING RAINS

*by Major Michael Halt*

·····································— ⁓⁓ —·····································

The order had come down at last. The ground invasion of Kuwait was about to commence. My battalion would cross the Kuwaiti border as part of Operation Desert Storm. I was the second in command of 130 brave marines who were about to face the most daunting challenge of their military lives.

We'd already dodged heavy artillery fire and now we'd likely face more dangers, like land mines and oil fires. Thousands of Iraqi troops waited just beyond the Kuwaiti border. It was time for us to make the final strategic push. *Dear God*, I prayed, *help me to lead my troops wisely. Watch over us. Keep us safe.*

I walked from one group of marines to another, talking to them about the mission and trying to keep their spirits up. Hunched against the dry, biting desert winds, we wrote letters home. Maybe our last.

Just before dawn the next morning I gave the order to move out. The skies were clear. We slung our gear into our Humvees and began advancing toward the border.

I felt a drop of rain, then another. In a matter of minutes it was pouring. The rain came down hard and fast, so thick we could barely make out the desert landscape ahead of us.

It went on for days. Each morning we'd awaken soaked to the bone after another night with only camouflage netting for cover. Bad enough we had the enemy to worry about. Now the elements were against us too. *Father, please make this rain stop and protect us.*

The rain continued to pound us relentlessly until we finally neared the Kuwaiti border. There the battalion halted. On the other side, the enemy waited. Rain or no rain, we'd soon be going in.

We awoke on the day of the invasion to clear skies and glorious sunshine. As we closed in on the border, we couldn't help but stare at the astounding sight before us. The torrential rains had washed away the sand to reveal metal disks planted all across our path. It was an Iraqi minefield.

# 3

# EXTRAORDINARY REASSURANCE

Do not fear, for I am with you; do not be dismayed, for I am your God. I will strengthen you and help you; I will uphold you with my righteous right hand."

ISAIAH 41:10 NIV

———

*Dear Lord, thank You that we can run to You when life gets overwhelming. Reassure our hearts that You are in control of every circumstance.*

# THE COMFORT I NEEDED

*by Paulie Panek*

———— ◦◦◦ ————

*I* was going through a rough patch in my life and thought a weekend getaway to one of Minnesota's lakes might lift my spirits. I signed up for a retreat set up by my church. On the way we skirted the town of Brainerd, and a lonely stretch of road where my mom died in a terrible car accident when I was seventeen. Recalling that horrible day made me feel sad and more down than ever. The question that had haunted me for more than twenty years came back: *Did Mom die all alone?* I'd thought I could find comfort in the answer, but since no one was able to tell me what had happened, that answer never came. My prayers seemed in vain.

At the retreat center I was assigned a room with several other women. One of them, Terri, had come all the way to the retreat from Midland, Texas. "What brings you to Minnesota?" I asked her.

"My mother lived near Brainerd," she told me.

"Really? I used to live near there."

"Mom passed away four months ago," Terri said. "After the retreat I'm going to visit her grave."

I remembered how hard my first visit to my mother's grave had been. Even after all these years the grief felt fresh. My mom was still such a presence in my life that it almost felt as if I could never completely stop mourning her. I knew what Terri must be going through. Before we got ready for bed that night, I decided to tell her my story.

"A man lost control of his car, crossed the centerline, and hit my mom's car head-on," I said. "That's what I was told. I wasn't with her when it happened."

"When was that?" Terri asked.

"November of 1973."

Terri looked shocked. Then she took my hand. "Paulie, I was the first person to stop at the scene after the accident. I was young, but I remember your mother well. I held her hand and prayed until the paramedics took her away. I was there."

Mom had not been alone. At last I had the answer, and the comfort I was searching for.

# Emma's Poster

### by Glen Liesegang

My wife, Linda, and I tried for years to conceive. Finally, at age forty, Linda got pregnant. She gave birth to a girl, whom we named Holly. We loved our daughter dearly. And we wanted her to have a brother or sister to grow up with.

Conceiving again was unlikely, so we looked into adoption. A close friend who's an obstetrician put us on a list of potential adoptive parents at our local hospital. Linda kept Holly's toys and clothes in hopes of having another child. But the years passed, and it didn't happen.

Linda was browsing in a bookstore one day when a children's poster caught her eye. Holly, six, was too old for it, but it would be perfect for a nursery. Linda put the poster in the closet with the other baby things. Maybe one day . . .

Early one morning, two years later, our friend, the obstetrician, called. "One of my patients, a college student, just decided to give up her baby for adoption," he said. "She asked me to help find a good family. You were the first ones I thought of."

On the way to the hospital, Linda said, "I know God brought us this baby for a reason, but I'm worried about our being new parents again at our age."

I tried to reassure her. "We just have to have faith that this is right."

At the hospital a nurse led us to a beautiful baby girl. "This is Emma," she said. "Well, that's our nickname for her."

"Emma," Linda repeated, taking the baby in her arms. "That's beautiful. She looks like an Emma."

Several days later we brought Emma home. We hurried to set up a nursery. I put together Holly's old crib and Linda rummaged through the closet for the baby things she'd tucked away. Underneath a stack of clothes Linda found the poster she had bought years earlier. She unrolled it and gasped.

"What is it?" I asked. Linda pointed to the picture. It showed a mother and daughter kneeling by a bed saying their evening prayers together. Beneath it there was a caption. It read, "Emma and Mommy talk to God."

# A Reason to Shout for Joy

*by Mary L.*

———— ⁑ ————

*I* sat in our living room, numb and devastated. I'd just told my husband to leave. I loved him, but I couldn't take his drinking anymore. All the broken promises and bitter words. All the failed attempts at change. I'd done everything I thought was within my power to help him. I'd even attended Al-Anon, a twelve-step support group for family and friends of alcoholics. But after twenty years, his drinking had finally destroyed our marriage.

While he was packing his things, I had to get out of the house. A woman I'd met in Al-Anon, who'd reached out to me as a sponsor, lived only a short walk away. I set off down the street, my hands buried in my coat pockets, my gaze fixed on the pavement. To my relief she was home. She poured me a cup of tea and listened to the all-too-familiar details. Then she said,

"I was thinking of you when I was reading my Bible this morning. One passage in particular spoke to me. I don't know why but it seemed meant for you."

"What was it?" I asked.

She opened her Bible and turned to chapter 3, verses 14–15 of Zephaniah (NAS), a book in the Old Testament that I hardly knew. Together we read: "Shout for joy, O daughter of Zion! . . . The King of Israel, the Lord, is in your midst; you will fear disaster no more." *Shout for joy?* I wondered. *When my heart is broken?*

The following months were the hardest of my life. I went to my Al-Anon meetings and spent time with my friend. I heard my husband was going to AA. He got in touch with me and convinced me that he was dealing with his problem. He'd taken his last drink. The night he moved back home I prayed for some reassurance, some sign that this was a true new beginning, not one more false step.

The next day we went to church. We sat together, our hands barely touching. Then the reading was announced, an obscure passage that I'd only seen months before. Now I listened in wonder to the words: "Shout for joy, O daughter of Zion! . . . You will fear disaster no more." That verse had been my promise. I didn't have to fear. And in the years since, my husband has never taken another drink.

# U R Going 2 B OK

*by Barbara Meader*

———〰———

*I*t was the middle of the night. My bedroom was still and dark, but I had barely slept a wink. Again. With every tick of the clock on my nightstand, my fear resounded in my head: *I'll never find a job! Never!*

I'd been laid off six months earlier. The bills were piling up and my unemployment benefits were about to run out. I'd sent out dozens of résumés, but I hadn't landed as much as an interview. Was there no hope for me? No light at the end of the tunnel?

*Please, God, give me peace*, I asked. *Let me get a little sleep!* But not even prayer brought me comfort. Finally I threw back the covers and shuffled to the bathroom to get myself a drink of water.

As I was standing at the sink, I heard my cell phone vibrating. My heart jumped. Who would call at this hour? It must be an emergency. I rushed to pick up the phone.

Too late. "Missed call," the display read. I didn't recognize the number. That was odd.

I sent the caller a text: "Who is it?"

Immediately a reply popped up on my phone. "LOL. It was a misdial, Barbs. Sorry."

Barbs. Only a few friends called me that. If someone was playing a joke on me, it wasn't funny. I couldn't imagine any friend of mine pulling this kind of trick. Annoyed, I sent another text: "You seem to know me, but I don't know you. I thought there was an emergency."

I held the phone and waited for a reply. It turned out it was a wrong number. The caller had gotten my voice mail first and that's how she knew my name. Then she finished the message. "Don't worry, Barbara," she texted. "There is a light that shines even in the night."

I looked at the message for a long moment before I got back into bed. *There is a light that shines even in the night.* I was going to be okay. Soon I drifted into a peaceful sleep. They had been the very words I needed to hear.

I eventually got a job. My mystery caller had the right number after all. There *was* an emergency that dark night—my crisis of faith.

# CHRISTMAS IN HURON

*by Robert Reynolds*

———

Huron, Ohio, was where I'd spent my twenties, working on a steamer out on the Great Lakes. My wife and I started our family there, and later we came back to Huron to retire. Then, during the final stages of construction on our new home, I had difficulty breathing. The doctor determined I needed open-heart surgery. I was admitted to a hospital in Sandusky. Everything was put on hold.

The night before my surgery, I was so worried I couldn't sleep. I lay in my hospital bed, praying and thinking about the events in my life that had led me to this point. I remembered how I had fallen in love with Huron and its people. I remembered a Christmas many years ago . . .

The shipping season had been good to me, so that winter I decided to buy some Christmas gifts and help out a family in town. "I know a family that would appreciate a visit from Santa Claus," the owner of the marine supply store said. "A woman with six children just lost her husband."

The store owner and his wife helped me wrap some presents and gave me the family's address. That evening I delivered the packages. A little girl with sparkly brown eyes and the sweetest smile answered the door. "Santa asked me to bring these gifts to you and your family," I said. The girl's eyes lit up even more. "Tell Santa thank you from Dorothy," she said. I never saw her or her family again, but they, and the other folks I met in town, helped give Huron a permanent place in my heart. A heart that now needed fixing, badly.

A nurse came in to check on me. "Will you pray with me?" I asked. She took my hand and held it until our prayer was finished.

"Where are you from?" she asked.

"Huron," I answered proudly.

She smiled. "I grew up there," she said. "I loved it, even though life wasn't easy. I lost my father when I was just a child."

I looked into her sparkly brown eyes and knew I'd seen them before. "Do you recall a sailor bringing presents to your door one Christmas?"

She stared. "That was you!"

"Yes, Dorothy," I said, suddenly confident about my surgery. "That was me."

# Meant to Be

### by Ginger Lingo

———⁂———

*M*ore than anything I wanted a new bike. I dreamed about it every day while walking to school. My father was a pastor so we didn't have much money. The only way I was going to get that bike was to earn my own money for it. So I worked hard, doing odd jobs like babysitting, weeding, and raking leaves. I stashed every penny I earned from those jobs and my allowance in my piggy bank.

Then one day at Sunday school our teacher told us of a letter she had received from Chile about a boy who had hepatitis. His missionary parents said he was recovering, but his spirits were still low. "Can you think of anything that might cheer him up?" our teacher asked us.

"A new bike!" the whole class exclaimed eagerly, and we agreed we would raise the money.

All week long I agonized over what to do. My conscience could only come up with one answer—give up my savings for the boy in Chile. So I emptied out my piggy bank and brought every cent to Sunday school. It was the hardest thing I had ever done, and maybe that's why it felt so right.

In college years later I found myself praying for something even harder than I had prayed for the bike—a man meant just for me. All my friends were dating. Why wasn't I? Was God asking me to wait again?

At last I met someone named Steve. We had a lot in common. He went to the college where my father taught, and my roommate was engaged to his best friend. He was earnest, smart, and hardworking. But I couldn't help wondering, *Is he really the one?*

One evening our families got together for dinner, a chance for everybody to get to know each other better. Over dessert and coffee Steve's mother talked about some of the places they had lived when they were missionaries. "Once when we were in Chile," she said, "Steve got hepatitis. You know what cheered him up?"

Of course I knew. He got a bike—my bike. And I got the husband I have been married to for twenty-nine years.

# ONE LAST TREAT

*by Judy Dill*

———— ∿ ————

Tom, my second husband, had a deep appreciation for the bond I had with my grown daughter from my first marriage. He loved treating Kris and me to a girls' day out and got a kick out of the giggle fits we got into when we recounted our day for him. He'd have to join us one day, we said. Shortly after we were married, he was diagnosed with melanoma. The treatments left him too weak to go out with us, but he never stopped exhorting us to have a good time. Two days shy of our second anniversary, he passed away. I felt a part of me had died too, that joy had gone from my life.

A few weeks after the funeral I tried to clean out Tom's dresser drawers. I thought I could handle it, but I was wrong. These were his favorite shirts, sweaters. Even a drawer full of change he'd emptied from his pockets made my heart ache. I sorted the coins, my eyes blurred with tears. Kris knew I needed a break. "Let's get out of the house, Mom," she urged. "We'll spend the day together. A girls' day out." A movie, dinner, something to get my mind off my grief.

We went to the bank to exchange the coins from Tom's drawer, then headed over to the theater. We bought two tickets, some snacks and drinks. "Twenty-eight dollars," the cashier announced.

Wow! "When did a trip to the movies get so expensive?" I exclaimed.

Kris giggled. "It's not five cents for a double feature anymore, Mom."

The movie helped push my thoughts elsewhere for a while. Afterward, we took Kris's dogs to the park and later we ate dinner at a casual restaurant. Spending the day with Kris was exactly what I needed. I just wished Tom could have been a part of it.

I got the check and tacked on a nice tip for our waiter. It came to thirty-eight dollars and thirty cents in total. As we walked to the car, a thought stopped me in my tracks. No, it can't be . . .

"What is it, Mom?" Kris asked. I reached into my pocket and pulled out the receipt from the bank. The coins in Tom's drawer added up to sixty-six dollars . . . and thirty cents.

For the first time since the funeral, I felt joy. I looked up toward the darkening sky, filling up slowly with stars. "Thanks, Tom," I said, "for treating us one more time."

# GRACE AND GLORY

*by Marie Bowen*

———— ⟋⟍ ————

On the day before her eighty-eighth birthday my mother fell at her assisted-living facility and suffered a concussion and multiple strokes. Thank God she survived. But her mental and physical abilities were severely limited. I flew from my home in Dallas to the facility in San Antonio to be with her. I knew I couldn't stay forever, but I wanted to. Mom had always been there for me. *Can the staff here take good care of my mother now that she's so helpless?* I worried. I didn't want to leave without knowing Mom was in good hands.

I slept in the room with her for two days, and still my worries hadn't stopped. On the third morning, sitting in a chair by her bed, I began to pray. Long ago my mother had taught me not to ask God for what I wanted, but to ask instead for His strength and guidance. "Where You lead me, I will follow," I prayed.

It made me think of that old hymn, "Where He Leads Me, I Will Follow." The tune got stuck in my head. "Where He leads me, I will follow..." I began to hum out loud. How'd the rest of it go? Oh yes: "He will give me grace and glory; he will give me grace and glory." Singing those words in my head comforted me. Grace and glory. I couldn't let my worries shake my faith. I would just have to trust that Mom would be okay, as hard as that was.

Just then, there was a knock on the door. Two nurse's aides walked in. "We're here to help your mother take a bath and get her ready for the day," one of them said. They took my mother gently by the hand and helped her out of bed, making sure she got her footing before they led her to the bathroom. All the while, the aides talked to my mother like a person, not a patient. I was impressed by how professional and kind they were. How could I have not appreciated the staff here before?

When they were done with Mom, the aides turned to leave. "Wait a minute," I said. "I just want to thank you two for taking such good care of my mom."

"You're welcome," one of the aides said. "If your mom needs anything, we'll be here."

"I'm Gracie," the other aide said. "And this is Gloria."

# Message in a Tree

*by Thelma Ganyon*

————— ✺ —————

*I* have a thing about hearts, believing there's a special reason for the shape. I've collected a lot of them. Some are store-bought—a heart-shaped muffin pan, shelves inlaid with little hearts, other knickknacks. The ones I'm really crazy about, though, are the hearts people give me that they happen to stumble upon. My kids bring me heart-shaped rocks, potatoes, leaves, shells, even a heart shape in the side of a freshly baked waffle (couldn't keep that one!). My husband, Richard, gets in on the act too. Once he shared a scrap of steel shaped like a heart that he found at his welding job. Every time I see hearts, I believe they're showing God's love to me.

That's what I needed a lot more of right now. We had just moved to North Carolina from Maryland with our two youngest children, and I was looking forward to a more relaxing lifestyle in our beautiful new home by the beach. But things weren't going as planned. Richard couldn't find welding work right away. Instead of relaxing, my part-time job as a receptionist had become full-time. And the kids were having problems adjusting to their new school.

One chilly afternoon I was outside with Richard, watching him chop wood for our fireplace. I recited my growing list of complaints. "Things just don't feel right here yet," I fussed. Richard lifted the ax above his head and came down on the tree limb with a heavy blow. He was probably sick of my complaining. I knew I was.

Richard stopped his chopping and waved me over. "Honey, come here," he said. *Now what's gone wrong?* I wondered, trudging over.

"Things are going to be just fine," he said. "You just need a reminder..."

He handed me the piece of wood he had been chopping. I turned it around in my hands. My heart stopped.

"Look," he said, pointing. Inside the limb, the cut revealed a hole...

It wasn't long before Richard found work, and the kids learned to love their new school. And I was finally able to relax. Whenever I think to complain now, I look at the slice of wood Richard saved for me. A reminder that God always cares...a heart-shaped hole He placed inside a tree branch. What a place to hide a love note!

# HUGGED

*by Pepper Helms*

———✺———

*I* wasn't looking forward to substituting at the pre-school that morning. Five months had passed since my two-year-old daughter, Hannah, had died, and I knew it would be hard for me to be around kids her age. I only said yes after the preschool director promised to assign me to the class of older kids. But I couldn't help feeling the emptiness around me as I drove to the school without Hannah. I longed to feel one of her big hugs, letting me know that everything would be okay.

Somehow, I managed to make it through the morning session. Before I knew it, it was time for re-cess. I brought the class into the gym. *So far, so good*, I thought. That's when I saw them—the class of two-year-olds walking in right behind us. A bunch of the younger kids started running around, playing with a kickball. I watched a girl I had never seen before chase the ball across the floor. Her hair was light brown and long with bangs, just like my daughter had had. *Hannah should be here too*, I thought. *She should be playing with these kids*. I fought to hold back the tears. I just missed her so much.

Suddenly the ball bounced away from the kids and rolled toward me. The little girl took off after it, her arms outstretched. But as the ball rolled past me, the girl didn't follow. Instead, she turned toward me.

*What does she want?*

I knelt down and the little girl came over to me, wrapped her arms around me and gave me a big, long bear hug. I was so stunned I couldn't react. I just closed my eyes. For a moment, I was feeling the fierce warmth of Hannah's embrace once again. Finally, she let go. "Thank you so much, sweetheart," I managed to say. "What's your name?"

"Hannah," she said. Could God have touched me in a more perfect way?

# IN GOD'S HANDS

## by Grace Booth

———⚬———

*I* was feeling pretty low. It was the week before I was scheduled for gallbladder surgery, and I couldn't escape my worried, gloomy thoughts. The surgeon was highly recommended but was new to me—and he didn't have the best bedside manner. My sister, an experienced operating room director, who usually put my mind at ease about my medical care, had moved away recently. This would be my first time facing an operation without her right there by my side.

I was on my own. *What if something goes wrong?* I tossed and turned all that night.

The next day I decided I had to get my mind off of everything. *A good book, that'll do the trick*, I thought. I headed to the bookcase in my guest bedroom to get something to read. Next to the bookcase was a stack of novels I had picked up from a library sale over a year ago and had not gotten around to putting away.

Right on top I spied a best-selling mystery novel. *This will keep me distracted*, I thought. Mysteries are my guilty pleasure.

I sat down in the bedroom, opened the book, and began to read. I couldn't believe it—the book's prologue began with a woman awaiting surgery! She was also feeling worried, struggling with knowing if she had chosen the right hospital, the right doctor.

"This is a team effort," the doctor assures her. "We mustn't forget someone very important," he continues, "the most important member of our team. Do you know who that is?"

I read on, breathless.

The doctor pats the woman's hand gently and points upward. "God," he tells her.

That doctor's words stopped me cold. The connection couldn't have been stronger or the circumstances more real to me.

My life wasn't only in the doctor's hands, it was in God's as well. Just the words that I needed to hear. Immediately I felt more confident and hopeful about the upcoming surgery.

And the most amazing thing? The character's name. It was the same as mine—Grace.

# Reassurance from Micah

*by Stephanie Thompson*

........................... ⟿ ...........................

$\mathcal{A}$ friend of mine cautioned me about giving birth at the health center near my home. "They don't have a neonatal unit," she said. "If anything goes wrong they'll have to rush the baby to Oklahoma City while you stay behind." I knew pregnancy at age forty could be risky, but I'd done everything I was supposed to: eaten healthy, read all the books, gone to childbirth classes. My doctor said I was doing fine. And the health center was smaller; I'd get more personalized attention there. So I ignored my friend's advice.

Meanwhile, my husband, Michael, and I thought about names. We knew we were having a girl; we decided to name her Micah. My husband liked it because the name was so close to his own. I liked it because of a verse in the book of Micah: "What does the Lord require of you but to do justice, and to love kindness and to walk humbly with your God?" We'd be blessed to have a daughter who embraced those qualities.

Throughout my term, I kept that verse in mind.

Four weeks before my due date, I began leaking fluid. Fearing the worst, I dialed my doctor immediately. "Call the health center and tell them you're coming in," she said. "I'll meet you there." But when I phoned the health center, they told me they were completely full.

"Looks like it's Oklahoma City after all," Michael said. The whole drive there I worried. *I did everything right*, I thought. *Why is this happening to me? Will my daughter be okay?*

Michael dropped me off in front of the hospital and then went to park the car. I walked into the atrium to wait for him. This place was so big, so impersonal. I put my hands on my belly and wondered what would happen next. Just then I noticed the sun coming through the skylight. I looked up and something caught my eye.

There, painted up near the ceiling, were words that soothed all my fears. I knew my daughter would be fine. The words? Micah 6:8, the same verse I'd held tight to throughout my pregnancy.

# Eye on the Sparrow

*by Josephine Novello*

———— ·✺· ————

Did you ever have the curious sensation that God was speaking to you? Not out loud, but with some beautiful, out-of-the-way gesture?

I had that feeling at a memorial service for my dear octogenarian friend Elisabeth Moore. This wonderful woman had lost her husband very soon after their wedding, and in all the years after that she never re-married. She dedicated her whole life to caring for people who needed her, especially children whom she liked to pretend she "adopted."

At one point in the service for her, the organ played "His Eye Is on the Sparrow," and as a soloist began to sing, a tiny sparrow flew in through an open window. Three times it circled the church ceiling, and then flew out. The sight of it caused my skin to tingle. To me it seemed that the Lord was using that sparrow to tell us that He, too, was well pleased with the lovely Elisabeth. I felt a sense of awe.

Only later, talking to one of her "adopted" children, now grown, did I learn that "His Eye Is on the Sparrow" was Elisabeth's favorite song. But, checking back, we discovered that no one had requested it to be sung: It was just coincidence that the organist had chosen it.

Coincidence?

# ONE RED ROSE

*by Eva Mae Ramsey*

———— ✶ ————

When my husband's sister Muriel became very ill, my husband and six-year-old daughter, Linda, and I traveled to Tulsa to be present while Muriel underwent emergency surgery for a diseased kidney. As we neared Tulsa, a thought flashed into my mind out of nowhere. *One red rose*, a voice said. *Take one red rose to Muriel*. My husband agreed to stop at a florist's shop. However, it was late and everything was closed.

The next morning my husband went to the hospital to wait during the operation. I stayed with Linda and my husband's elderly mother at her home. All I could think of was that one red rose. I felt compelled to search out that rose. So Linda and I walked uptown, and I bought one red rose.

When my husband returned, he said that Muriel had come through the surgery, and it was now touch-and-go as to whether she'd recover. He also told me he'd ordered a big bouquet of gladiolus for Muriel's room.

"That's lovely, honey," I said. "But she's got to have this red rose, too." When we went to the hospital later, Muriel was still groggy and wasn't able to talk to us, but I put the rose, by itself, in a vase where she could see it. Because of work commitments we had to return home without ever talking to Muriel, but we did learn that she would recover.

Soon we got a letter. "Before I went to the hospital," Muriel wrote, "I prayed that if I was supposed to live, God would send me a sign I specifically asked for, something that meant God was with me and would give me the heart to go on. When I opened my eyes after the operation, there it was, the very thing I'd prayed for—a red rose."

# Light in My Loneliness

### by Arthalyn Kublick

Something was wrong with our basement light. I had to wiggle the switch repeatedly to get it to work, and even then, more often than not, the light didn't come on at all. "Don't worry," my husband, Dan, said, "I'll take care of it." I believed him. Dan built that house—put up the walls and roof, did most of the wiring and plumbing himself.

The house was comfortable, one sunny floor and a basement that included Dan's shop and my own workroom. Those four cozy walls were our warmth during the long, harsh Canadian winters near Minitonas—a small town three hundred miles northwest of Winnipeg.

Busy every day, Dan didn't get around to the switch. Besides work in the house, he had equipment to keep up, bees and cattle to tend, and farming to do. It didn't help that his back was bothering him.

Once, he'd been able to do it all with no problem. But now, for some reason he tired easily, and his back hurt so badly that he couldn't lie down. Worried, we saw a doctor. Dan was diagnosed with cancer.

Soon I was spending my weekends in Dan's hospital room in Winnipeg. During the week, I continued to carry out my duties as a kindergarten teacher back home in Minitonas. The house was so empty. Every time I peered down the stairs into the basement, I felt as if the darkness were going to swallow me. *I know You are with me, Lord, but I feel so alone.*

After Dan died, I hardly knew what to do with myself. The thought of going down to the basement only made me feel worse. But I saw I couldn't avoid it. There was work to be done, and anyway, our deep freezer was down there.

The first time I opened the door at the top of the steps after Dan's death, I paused and drew in a breath. I reached over and flipped the switch. The light went on immediately. It has worked perfectly ever since.

No, Dan never got around to fixing that switch. But Someone did take care of it, Someone who fills all our emptiness with light.

# Locket of Love

*by Donna Bosman*

My husband, Harvey, and I were visiting Ashland, Wisconsin, when I spotted a secondhand store. I coaxed Harvey into going inside with me. He didn't have much patience for antique shopping, but I loved poking around old shops, looking for that unexpected treasure. My eyes took in the clutter—a monogrammed silver baby cup, a guitar with no strings, a wedding dress that was advertised as "never used"— while Harvey stood near the door, waiting.

I was drawn to a glass case filled with beautiful old jewelry—rings, bracelets, brooches, and a small gold locket. It took me back to when I was young and my father was frequently away on business. He always brought home a few little gifts. Once he returned from a long sales trip with a gold locket for Mom and, as always, a big hug for me.

That was long ago. Mom was gone and Dad had died twenty years back. Toward the end of his life Dad and I had a terrible disagreement. We never patched things up. If only I'd had one last chance to say I loved him, to feel his arms around me. I often told myself that there was no reason to cling to this sadness. Just as often, I'd find myself asking God for assurance that somehow my father had not died thinking I didn't love him.

"Could I see that locket?" I said to the salesclerk. He took it from the case and I ran my thumb over its surface, worn smooth by the years. I started to open it when I heard Harvey clear his throat. "How much?" I asked the clerk quickly. "Ten dollars," he said.

"I'll take it," I replied, tugging a ten-dollar bill from my purse. "Just a second, dear," I said to Harvey. The clerk smiled as he put the locket back in its box and handed it to me. "Enjoy."

In the car I finally got a chance to examine the locket. I clicked it open with a fingernail and gasped at what I saw. A tiny black-and-white photo of my father that he'd given to my mother years ago. It was the very same locket I remembered. A gift that expressed his love all the more the second time around.

# 4

# EXTRAORDINARY RECOVERIES

In that day they will say, "Surely this is our God; we trusted in him, and he saved us. This is the Lord, we trusted in him; let us rejoice and be glad in his salvation."

ISAIAH 25:9 NIV

⸺ ⁓ ⸺

*Lord, nothing is too difficult for You. Thank You for caring about the minutest details of our lives!*

# The Tornado and the Tome

*by Helen Walsh Folsom*

························ —ᴠᴠᴠ— ························

We'd just come home from church, my daughter Bettse and I. We dropped our purses on the dining room table, ate some pizza for lunch, and sat down on the couch to watch TV. I looked out the window. The sky was a sickly gray, the horizon almost yellow. We'd made it back just in time.

But then a loud wail started up in the distance. "The sirens!" Bettse exclaimed. A second later, an alert flashed on the TV. A tornado was heading right toward us. "Quick, come on," I shouted to Bettse. Living here in Kansas, we knew what to do. We dashed to the sturdiest part of the house, the bathroom. No time to grab anything. I didn't even have time for prayer. We barely shut the bathroom door when the whole house started to tremble. The air rushed out of the room. I crouched on the floor and shut my eyes, holding onto a water pipe with all my strength. With a loud roar, glass shattered and wood cracked all around us. Dust and debris rained down on top of me. Wind and rain whipped at my face. Then, as quickly as that, it was all over.

I opened my eyes. Through the dust I saw the cloudy sky above, peeking through a gaping hole in the roof. I tried to stand, but pieces of the wall and ceiling pinned me down—I couldn't move. "Don't worry, Mom, I think I can get help," Bettse said. She stood on a stool and shouted out the hole to some neighbors. They came running, and carefully lifted the bathroom wall off of me so I could scoot out. *It's a miracle we're alive*, I thought, looking at the house. The southwest corner was gone. My checkbook and credit cards, my important files! Then it struck me: My bookcase was nowhere to be seen. *Dear Lord, no. Not the book too!*

Not just any book, mind you. It was my most-prized possession. Five years earlier, after a career working as a newspaper columnist, I decided to devote myself to writing full-time about Ireland. It felt like a calling to me. Nothing fascinated me more than my family's Irish heritage. My great-grandmother Lizzie Walsh came over from Ireland in 1849, part of the great tragic wave from the Irish famine. My grandfather's Scotch-Irish family came to the United States before the Revolutionary War. I scrounged used bookstores and garage sales for old volumes on Irish culture and history, the older and more tattered the better.

One day I dropped by a small, friendly bookstore I'd been to often. "Have you got any more Irish books for me?" I asked. The little lady smiled. "Well, we have this one; we're not sure what to do with it. It needs repairs."

She brought out a large box. Inside was a book about the size of a VCR, and even heavier. I lifted off the loose cover. The illustrated color frontispiece was still bright; the pages were yellowed but intact. My heart soared when I recognized the title—it was a book I'd seen referenced in so much of my research: *The Annals of Ireland of the Four Masters*.

In 1632, three Irish writers and one monk in Donegal risked their lives to secretly record Ireland's history, an act forbidden by the conquering English who were determined to assimilate them. The writers and monk recorded names, dates, and facts from long before Christ, rich with descriptions of Ireland's people, their legends, and culture. The book in front of me was a first edition of the translation into English, printed in 1846. A treasure that had practically fallen into my lap, right here in the middle of Kansas. It was as though God were blessing me in my new career. I bought it on the spot.

With the help of my treasured tome, I wrote two books over the next four years about Irish history and culture. When I wasn't using it for research I kept it wrapped in a white pillowcase on the top shelf of the bookcase.

But now it was gone. And almost everything else with it. My late husband had built this house with his own two hands, and my daughter and I still lived here, in a deep, wooded valley on the outskirts of Kansas City. Now I sat on a broken chair, staring at the remains. The gas heater had ripped off the pipes and had been thrown over the house onto the hill. The TV, beds, and an armoire were gone entirely. Bedding and clothing were scattered into the trees off to the northeast. Broken gas lines hissed and torn wires sent flashes of sparks wherever they touched. *Where do I begin, Lord?* I wondered. It was as if some ancient giant of Celtic lore had reached from the sky and torn my life asunder in a matter of seconds.

Police, firemen, and rescue workers came and went. But they had six hundred other homes to cover, victims of the same tornado. Still in shock,

Bettse and I went to my brother-in-law's place. We all watched the news that night and saw the destruction the tornado had caused—the worst I'd ever seen, like a huge buzz saw had cut across our county.

We couldn't get to our house for two days. All the while I prayed, *God, give me some sign that there's still hope.* Finally, Bettse and I went back with my son, Bill, my nephew, and his wife to salvage anything we could find. I stood outside. It didn't seem like much was left. My nephew found our door frame and a piece of the wall three blocks away, in the woods. His wife plucked a few ruined shirts out of the trees. *It looks like I've lost everything, Lord.*

"Mom, look!" Bill called. I made my way inside the house. He was holding two purses, Bettse's and mine, found under the broken dining room table. Elsewhere in the rubble we found my file cabinet, mangled, drawers jutting out, empty. Except the top one. It was shut tight. I opened it—my insurance papers and bank records! *Thank You, Lord.*

"Yes!" I heard Bettse shout from the other room. She held up her watch, bracelet, and ring looped together, found lying on the floor in the debris.

I looked at that empty space where the bookshelf once stood. The news reports said that people were finding shredded objects picked up from the tornado almost a hundred miles away. Was there any hope of finding my beloved book? I went outside and wandered around aimlessly. I walked past our battered cars, stumbling over broken tree limbs.

For some reason I looked up at a tree not too far away. I walked over. Something white was dangling from a branch, oddly as if it had been placed there. A shirt maybe? I extended my arms as far as they would go. I could just reach it, and gave it a tug. It came tumbling from the tree, right into my arms. It wasn't a shirt. It was a pillowcase, *the* pillowcase, the book nestled securely inside! The *Annals* was still whole and undamaged! As safe as the day I got it.

There's an old Irish saying: "May you be poor in misfortune and rich in blessings." Standing there that day in the midst of all that misfortune, I felt so very, very rich.

# GRANDMA'S OLD CHAIR

## by Beverly Palmer

—⁂—

"What do you regret, Beverly?" one of my friends in our Christmas caroling group asked me at our church meeting. I'd just joined that year and we were bonding, talking about things we wished we might have done differently in our lives.

There wasn't much that I would change. I believe everything happens for a reason. But there was one thing. "It may seem silly...," I said.

My grandmother and grandfather were like my other set of parents. Often after school I would walk over to their house and sit in my favorite chair in their living room. The chair always fascinated me—even though its striped upholstery was faded and it had nicks here and there in its wooden legs and arms. The arms were carved with ornate circles that I liked to trace with my fingers. Sitting in that chair, I felt safe. I would relax, have a snack, and chat with Grandma and Grandpa until my parents came home.

After my grandparents died, that chair was passed down to me. I brought it to my new home when I married.

Years later, however, my husband and I found ourselves in tough times. We wanted to buy a swing set for our two young sons, so we held a yard sale. I knew of one item that would definitely sell well: my grandparents' antique chair. It killed me, but I wanted to make the kids happy. The chair fetched a nice price, and we were able to buy the swing set. But when we moved out of town the following year, I felt like I'd left a part of my family behind. I felt that way now, even after all this time.

"That was"—I thought about how old the boys were now—"twenty-two years ago," I recalled. "And even though it's been so long, I still think about my grandparents' chair."

Two of the ladies looked at each other with obvious amazement. "Beverly," one of them said, "there's something you should see . . ."

At their urging, I went downstairs to the church basement. It was almost like walking into my grandparents' living room. There, sitting in front of me, was my chair, the striped lining, the carved circles in the armrests . . . even the nicks and dents I knew so well.

# Long-Lost Family

*by Joan M. Bark*

———•———

My parents split up when I was only six months old, and Mom got so upset at the mere mention of my father that I didn't dare try to get in touch with him growing up. All I had of my dad were a few faded photographs, and I longed for something more, especially after I heard he'd remarried and had another daughter and a son. *I will find the rest of my family*, I told myself. *Someday.*

But the time just never seemed right. I married— happily, I'm grateful to say—and I put off my search because of Mom. When she died, Dad was already gone and with him, I feared, any link I had to my lost siblings.

I tried to fill the void in my life by volunteering for a mentoring program at a local school. Immediately I was drawn to Melissa, a fifth grader with freckles and an attitude. She acted tough, but I saw such sadness in her big brown eyes. "Want to talk?" I offered. Like she'd been waiting for the chance, she opened up about her problems at home. A nasty divorce, a bitter mom, a dad she longed to see more of . . . it sounded so familiar. Mentors weren't supposed to get involved in students' personal lives; we weren't even told their last names. Still I couldn't help growing closer to Melissa with my every visit to her classroom.

Too soon, school let out. All summer I wondered how Melissa was. But in the fall, I learned she'd moved away to live with her father. *I hope that she's happier.*

That winter my husband noticed in the paper the obituary of a woman with my maiden name. "Survived by her younger brother, Kenneth," it read. Could it be? I went to the funeral home.

The man greeting visitors was the image of my dad. I introduced myself to my half brother and told him how sorry I was about his loss. Once the initial shock wore off, he had me meet his son, Kenny Jr. Then he drew forward a little freckle-faced girl. "And this is your niece . . ." She looked up at me with wistful brown eyes. Melissa. My connection to my long-lost family was stronger than I knew.

# Dream Come True

*by Mary Frances Williams*

*I* sat up in bed and tried to clear my head. I dreamed I was visiting an older woman who said her name was Pearl. There in her living room was my old cedar chest. It had a sad history.

I hadn't laid eyes on that chest in more than thirty years. I would have recognized it anywhere, though. The simple lines, the delicate hinges, the clear finish that protected the beauty of the wood.

My father came from a long line of woodworkers. They had a tradition of welcoming each new baby in the family with a handmade cedar chest. Dad's uncle had hewn the cedar and crafted the chest just for me. It stood at the foot of my bed, a constant reminder to me of how much I was loved.

Then my parents had a bitter divorce, and Dad took my brothers to live with him. He threw their clothes into the chest and carried it out the door. With it, it seemed, went my best childhood memories.

*Come on, Frances,* I told myself. *Forget the dream. You've got to get to work.*

I was a volunteer services coordinator, and I'd booked a gospel choir from out of town to perform at our local hospital. I got there early to greet the choir. The members filed in. I could hardly believe my eyes—there was the woman from my dream!

"This is going to sound odd," I said to her. "I had a dream last night . . . and you were in it."

She smiled. "Really?"

I couldn't resist asking, "Your name wouldn't be Pearl, would it?"

Her eyes widened. "My name is Pearl."

"I was visiting you. You had a small chest sitting in your living room . . ."

"What did it look like?" Her expression turned serious.

"Natural cedar. Simple. Small hinges. Beautiful, clear finish. My dad took it with him when he left my mother."

She touched my arm. "Was your dad Earnest?"

"How did you know?"

"Your father was my cousin. One day he came by and gave me the chest for safekeeping. I held on to it all these years. Now I know why."

# The Letter That Made Its Way Back

*by Valarie Ripka*

———— ✳ ————

*I* didn't recognize the return address on the envelope I pulled from the mailbox. Probably junk mail, I thought, opening it. To my surprise, there were two letters inside. Intrigued, I unfolded one of them. "Dear Val," it began. *Dear Val?* I had no idea who the letter was from.

"I hope you don't mind that I have located you. Enclosed is a letter, but I had to send an explanation with it. Let me tell you a bit about myself...

"For the past several years, I have endured one struggle after another. The minute I get my head above water, something else pulls me under. Yesterday was one of those times. Going over some papers, I just put my head down and said, 'I cannot do this anymore.'

"The next morning, I went grocery shopping, and in the parking lot, I saw a folded sheet of paper on the ground next to my car. I thought it was some-one's grocery list, but something I saw made me pick it up. It was a letter . . .

"'Dear Becky,' it read. 'You have been on my mind and heart a lot because I know you are hurting.' The letter contained a poem, 'I Am Waiting, Lord,' about having faith through difficult times. 'Lord, help me not to simply sit among my broken things,' one line read. '. . . teach me in my waiting to find the valued remnants . . .'

"Even though I was not the person originally in-tended to receive this letter, I believe I was meant to see it. I do hope the other Becky got as much encourage-ment from it as I have. Thanks so much . . . Becky."

Slowly, I unfolded the other letter in the envelope, the one the writer had mentioned. And I did recognize the person who wrote this one. It was signed "Val Ripka." Me.

I had sent that letter to my friend Becky when she was going through a rough time in her life. It had comforted her back then, ten years earlier. She had thanked me for it when she'd received it, but later had told me that she had long since lost it, not sure where it might have gone.

Until it was found by just the right person, at just the right time.

# Mangled in the Garbage Disposal

*by Rose Vander Ark*

—⁓—

*I*t happened so fast. I was doing the dishes, the garbage disposal was rumbling and then . . . *clink!* I looked down in time to see a glint of gold vanish down the drain. My opal ring! I heard a sickening crunch. Quickly, I turned off the disposal. *Please let it be okay.* My ring couldn't be damaged, not again.

Many years earlier, the opal had cracked and I'd taken it to a jeweler. "The stone has to be replaced," he told me. "Fortunately, the setting is fine—it's truly unique," he went on, pointing out the flowers intricately carved on the gold band. "They don't design rings like this anymore." Then he smiled and said, "Don't worry; it'll be good as new."

Opal is my birthstone—October—and the ring was a twentieth birthday gift from my parents. Along with my engagement and wedding rings, it was my most treasured piece of jewelry.

The jeweler did a wonderful job. He replaced the opal and the ring looked brand new. "Never leave it on when putting your hands in warm, soapy water," he cautioned. "That's what may have caused the stone to crack in the first place."

For years I'd been so careful. I even mounted a cute heart-shaped ring holder on the wall by the sink to hang my ring on.

But today, the vibrations from the disposal had shaken the ring from the holder. Fighting back tears, I fished out a tiny lump of gold. My ring was mangled beyond recognition.

I drove to the kind jeweler who had fixed it before. But his store was gone. He'd clearly been out of business for some time. My heart sank. Without him, how could my ring ever be fixed?

I took it to a jeweler I knew from church. He examined the lump and shook his head. "I'm sorry," he said. "I don't know where to start. But I'll have my gemologist take a look at it."

He went to the back room. I looked sadly at the place on my finger where the ring had always been. Where it would never be again.

Moments later the gemologist came out. The same voice, the same smile, the same jeweler who'd fixed my ring years ago! "I remember this ring very well, because the setting was so unique," he said. "I can re-create it from memory."

# FAMILY ABROAD

*by Natalie Garibian*

························· —ᴍ— ·························

*I* was a college junior on my year abroad in Paris. It should have been wonderful. It wasn't. Everything was so different: the clothes, the food, the language. I longed for something—anything—familiar. My tight-knit Armenian family was in Florida, thousands of miles away.

One Sunday I called to say hi. Their voices on the telephone were the first familiar sounds I'd heard in weeks. I cried after I hung up. I'd never felt so home-sick before. If only I were close to someone here, I thought.

I took a walk across town. I'd passed the Armenian church in Paris many times before, but had never gone in. I realized that back in America, my family would be going to church too. Maybe being there now would make me feel closer to them.

I took a seat in the back pew just as the service started. I looked around. The priest, the prayers, the faces in the congregation—this church was a lot like my family's church in Florida. *For now, these people will be my family. Please, God, let me feel that.*

I looked up and saw an old woman coming slowly up the aisle, leaning heavily on a cane. I asked her—in Armenian—if she wanted to sit. She nodded and I slid over.

The old woman bowed her head, losing herself in prayer. I tried to pay attention to the service, but I couldn't keep my eyes off her. There was something familiar in her face; she could have been my own grandmother. But I didn't know this woman. She noticed me staring and smiled.

"You're not from here, are you?" she whispered.

"No," I said. "I come from the United States."

She nodded. After a moment, she said, "I've lost touch with them, but I used to have some nephews in America—in Florida. Sarkis, Dikran, and . . ."

A lump rose in my throat. I knew exactly what she was going to say.

"Ara," I finished. "Ara Garibian. My father."

The old woman took my hand. "*Asdudzo kordz,*" she whispered—*God's work.* "I am your great-aunt. We are family."

# LOST SOCKS

*by Mark E. Mize*

One winter I led a weekly Bible study in Shreveport, Louisiana. We always invited non-church members to come and join the discussion. One day I met Terri, a young nurse. She had been struggling with all sorts of things, and it seemed like she could use a bit of spiritual guidance. But the weeks passed, and she never came. "You should really try and make it," I urged her the next time I saw her.

"I'm not sure it's the right place for me," she said. I didn't want to be pushy, so I let it go.

Later that month I needed to pick up a few Christmas gifts, so I headed to the mall. After fighting the holiday crowds and getting my things, I got back into the car and pulled out of the parking space. Something was in front of me. I got out to take a closer look. It was a shopping bag from Dillard's department store—filled with a number of pairs of expensive-looking socks. I called up the store when I got home. "Did anyone lose their shopping bag full of socks?" They said no one had reported it. I gave them my number in case someone called looking for the bag. No one did.

A week later I was leading the Bible study when in walked Terri. She stayed very quiet the whole time, just sitting and listening as the rest of us discussed the passage we'd read. I hoped that there'd be something she'd show interest in, but she just looked sad.

At the end, like always, I asked if anyone had anything to share. "I'm sorry," Terri said, "I'm not sure if I believe in all that. Nothing's been going right for me. Work's been tough, I've had problems in my family, I'm single for the holidays . . . and I can't even shop for presents without something going wrong."

"What happened?" I asked.

"Last week I bought a gift for my dad, and somewhere between the store and home, it just disappeared—a whole bag of designer socks."

"Designer socks from Dillard's?" I asked. She nodded.

I smiled. "I think you've come to the right place."

# My Aunt June

## by Kathy Morrison

Aunt June was always there for me growing up. She wasn't really my aunt—she was one of my mother's best friends. But she was more like family. She saw me through dance recitals, first dates, and made sure I was well-polished in table manners and full of Southern charm. I loved to watch her knit, her hands deftly gliding the needle in and out, turning mere yarn into beautiful things. When I was pregnant with my first child, Aunt June told me she wanted to knit a blanket for my baby. But she never had the chance. She passed away that summer, a few months before my baby girl was born.

I thought about my aunt as I rocked my newborn in my arms. *Aunt June would've loved to be part of this,* I thought. I wished my baby could have felt the love and care that Aunt June had given to me for all those years.

Two years later I was expecting another child. I vowed that this time I would try to knit a blanket like Aunt June would have made.

One day, after a visit to the doctor, I ran to the local thrift store to buy some yarn. They had a used yarn bin that I would sometimes pick from. I dug around, looking for a bargain.

Then I saw it, a big bag of cream-colored yarn with a pair of needles—and it was only one dollar and ninety-eight cents! Someone had even started knitting a pattern for a blanket.

I bought it and headed home. I was so exhausted when I got back that I tucked the bag of yarn into the closet and forgot about it.

A few weeks later I planned to visit my mother. *I should bring that yarn with me; I'll have time to knit over there*, I thought. I reached into the closet and pulled out the bag.

When I took the yarn out at my mother's house, a piece of paper fell from the bag and fluttered to the floor. *What is that?* I wondered. I squatted down and picked it up.

It was a knitting pattern for a baby blanket. And in the corner, the person who started it had written her name: *June Gerst*. My aunt June.

# The Search

## by John Gleason

—⁂—

*I*t happened years ago, but the incident sticks in mind and memory. Perhaps I can make you see why.

It was October 1938. I had just graduated from Northwestern University and wanted to see something of the world before settling into a career. With $350 saved from a summer job—quite a lot in those days—I was heading for Puerto Rico and the Virgin Islands, places that seemed romantic to me.

In New York I boarded a rusty, old coal-burning freighter. At first there seemed to be just three passengers besides myself: a bright young civil engineer from Michigan, a worried-looking old man in a white linen suit, and a stately, charming woman who turned out to be Mrs. Charles Colmore, wife of the Episcopal Bishop of Puerto Rico, who was returning there after a visit to relatives in the United States.

We made friends quickly, the way you do on a sea voyage. Then, two days out of New York, a young woman with dull blonde hair appeared on deck for the first time. She was in her early twenties, much too thin. She looked so pale and wan that we instantly pitied her. She seemed a bit wary of us male passengers, but she accepted Mrs. Colmore's invitation for tea in her cabin.

"It's a strange story," the bishop's wife told us later. "She comes from a little town in Pennsylvania and she's on her way to the West Indies to look for her husband. He evidently left home several months ago after a violent quarrel with the girl's mother over his drinking and his inability to find a job and support his wife properly. The girl finally heard a rumor that her husband had gone to the West Indies. She still loves him, so she left her old dragon of a mother, and now she's on her way to find Billy—that's her husband's name: Billy Simpson."

"You mean," I said "she's going to leave the ship when we get to San Juan and start looking? Why, that's crazy! There are hundreds of islands in the Caribbean; maybe thousands."

"I told her that," the bishop's wife said, "but it didn't seem to make any impression. She just says she'll find him. How, I don't know. But she seems absolutely sure of it."

"It would take a miracle," the old man said, thin and intense in his white tropic suit and brown wool cap.

"It would take a whole hatful of miracles," I muttered.

"Does she have any friends where she's going?" asked the young engineer. "Does she have any money?"

"No friends," said the bishop's wife. "And almost no money. Ten dollars, I think she said. Not even enough to get her back to New York."

When we heard this, the rest of us dug into our pockets and raised twenty-five dollars to give to this strange waif of a girl.

"This will help you find a place to stay when we get to San Juan," the bishop's wife said when she presented the money in front of all of us. "And I'm sure our church there will help find enough for your return passage home."

The girl murmured her thanks. Then she said, "But I'm not going home. I'm going to find my husband."

"Where? How?" asked the old man.

The girl shrugged and smiled a little. She had the oddest smile—sad, fateful, dreamlike. "Prayers," she said. "My prayers. A few years ago, I asked God to send me someone to love, and He did, and I married him. Now I'm asking God to help me find my husband again. That's all. Just asking. And I'm sure He will."

The engineer turned away. "Not rational," he murmured, and I nodded. He was a tall, friendly fellow on his way to become a plantation overseer on Santo Domingo. He was a couple of years older than I, and it made me feel like a man of the world to agree with him. The old man said nothing. The bishop's wife looked thoughtful. We didn't discuss the matter again.

Time passed, trancelike, the way it does on shipboard. We docked in San Juan early one morning. I was scheduled to catch another boat that afternoon for St. Thomas in the Virgin Islands, and so had a few hours to kill. The others were going to look for an inexpensive hotel where the girl could stay while she figured out her next move, whatever that might be. The engineer and the old man needed a place to stay too. The bishop's wife had delayed her own trip to Ponce, where the bishop was, in order to give some reassurance to the girl. "I've got to see her settled somewhere," she said to me privately. "And then I'll ask some people at the church to keep an eye on her. She has this unshakable faith, and I've done some praying myself, but . . ."

"But she needs that hatful of miracles, doesn't she?" I said.

Mrs. Colmore smiled. "A great big hat," she said. "A God-sized one, perhaps."

In the smothering heat of midday we walked all over the old city of San Juan, finding the cheap hotels—all run-down establishments infested with fleas and bedbugs. Finally the bishop's wife suggested that we get on a bus for the little neighboring town of San Terce. She thought accommodations might be more attractive and more available there.

So we clambered onto a bus for San Terce, but all the hotels we found in this pleasanter suburb were too expensive. Finally, exhausted under the hot sun, the bishop's wife, the old man, and the girl sat down on a sidewalk bench. The young engineer and I continued the search and, amazingly, we found a pleasant, clean, and inexpensive hotel within a block.

We tried to register for the group, but the clerk insisted in broken English that each person register individually. So I went and brought the others into the lobby, where they lined up before the registration book. When it was the girl's turn to sign, she picked up the pen, glanced at the page, dropped the pen—and fainted.

The clerk dashed for some water. The engineer and I put the girl on a couch, and the bishop's wife bathed her forehead while the old man patted her hand. After drinking some water, she came to slowly.

"Heat too much for you?" I asked sympathetically.

She shook her head. "No . . . Billy."

"Billy?"

"He's in the book," the girl whispered.

We jumped up to take a look. There, scrawled after a date two days before, we read: "Billy Simpson."

"Billy Simpson! What room is he in?" I asked the clerk. I couldn't believe it.

"Simpson?" the clerk said. "Oh, he got a job. He come back after work. Not here now."

"This can't be," the old man said almost angrily when the clerk's description of Billy Simpson seemed to fit the girl's. "She must have had some idea that he was here!"

Still lying on the couch, the girl didn't hear, but the bishop's wife looked at us. "No, I'm sure she didn't," she said. "Otherwise she would have come directly to this hotel on her own, wouldn't she?"

Nobody could answer that. It was obvious that there could be no final answer until Billy Simpson came back from work—by which time I was supposed to be on the boat that sailed overnight to the Virgin Islands.

Now, I know that in a good story the narrator does not remove himself from the scene just when the climactic episode is coming up. But this is the way it all happened. I guess real life doesn't always write the script the way a good playwright would.

Anyway, I had to go. The engineer shook my hand and wished me well. The bishop's wife gave me a letter of introduction to the Episcopal minister on St. Thomas, a Reverend Edwards. The old man said he would come and see me off.

The boat for St. Thomas was belching smoke, more of a ferry than a ship. As we neared the gangway, the old man spoke. "The real reason I wanted to come along was to ask you something. Do you think that prayer really led that girl to her husband?"

"I don't know," I replied uneasily. "There's always coincidence. But this is certainly a big coincidence."

He took my arm. "I wonder if prayer could help me?" he said. "I just wanted to ask you. I don't know much about it."

"Neither do I," I said. "Why don't you ask the bishop's wife? She prayed for the girl, you know."

"Do you think I should? I've been a bit afraid to."

"Sure," I said. "Ask her. And if I hear of any jobs in the Virgin Islands, I'll write you at the hotel."

"Thanks," he said. "Have a good trip." He waved to me from the dock after I was aboard.

When I arrived, Reverend Edwards invited me to stay with him, charging only ten dollars a week for room and board. Settled in, I spent my time sightseeing, chatting with natives at the docks, writing, relaxing, learning all I could about the islands. Evenings I often visited with Reverend Edwards after dinner. One night I told him about the girl on the boat and the missing husband and the prayers, and probably my tone clearly indicated my doubts about it all.

The old clergyman said: "Don't ever be afraid to believe, John. You're too young to have a closed mind."

With time, the girl and Billy Simpson almost slipped from memory. But one day I mentioned the incident to two new friends of mine, deaconesses who lived next door to the church.

"Why," said one of them, "that Mr. Simpson sounds like a Mr. Simpson we had here at the church clinic. He came from Antigua with a very bad case of the DTs. We practically had to chain him to a bed."

"And then," said the other, "one day he suddenly became alert and insisted on getting up. Our Danish doctor said he'd better stay with us for a time, but Mr. Simpson was adamant. He said he had to get to San Juan to see someone. When we asked who, he said he didn't know. He just had to get to San Juan. That night he caught a small power boat going to Puerto Rico. We gave him twenty dollars to get him there and maybe enough for a room. That's the last we heard of him. Now this?"

We compared dates, and this "Mr. Simpson" would have landed in Puerto Rico three days before my group arrived in San Juan from New York. He could have reached that hotel two days before we had, as the register showed.

I had to find out. I wrote to the bishop's wife, gave her my news, and asked for hers. In two weeks, her answer came: "Yes, it was the right Billy Simpson. His reunion with his wife was one of the most touching things I've ever seen. Now, there have to be several events to consider, miracles possibly. One, Mr. Simpson's sudden cure from alcoholism in St. Thomas, which he confirms; two, his strange compulsion to get to San Juan, which he couldn't understand himself at the time; three, the guidance that led him to that particular hotel; four, his finding a good job within twenty-four hours, after not being able to get a job for months; five, the guidance that took our group to that hotel, a hotel which you yourself found. For me, these events add up to a hatful of miracles that can be explained in only one word: prayer. The Simpsons are living happily in San Juan now. Not long ago they gave me fifty dollars to use for charity, and so I am enclosing twenty dollars for your friends who helped Mr. Simpson while he was ill."

I sat with Mrs. Colmore's letter in my lap for a long time.

A week later, I received a letter from the old man. He had gone to Ponce with the bishop's wife, found a good job, joined the church, and become very happy in it. He wrote: "When we were all at the hotel that day, Mrs. Colmore said that maybe there was a lesson in the experience we had just shared. I believe there was. For me, the lesson was that some people instinctively know the power of prayer, but others have to learn it."

I couldn't argue with that.

These days, my mind is no longer so young, it is no longer closed, and I am no longer afraid to believe.

# Lost and Found

*by Charles Sweitzer*

When I entered the service during World War II, I was given a small, pocket-size New Testament with my name inscribed on the inside front cover. Often I read passages for comfort from the stresses of army life. But just before the invasion of Europe we were told we weren't allowed to have any personal identification with us other than our dog tags. Reluctantly I handed in my Bible.

I made my way safely through Normandy, then moved with the American troops across France into Holland, Belgium, and Germany. I often thought of my Bible, and when I prayed I could still remember God's promises written there.

At the war's end I returned to the States. Eventually I married and raised a family. One day my daughter Nancy called me; she and her Danish husband, Jorgen, had been unpacking after a recent move.

"One box was full of books," she said. "But I couldn't read a word of them because they were all written in Danish. So I asked Jorgen to look at them. He said they were hymnals he had bought ten years ago at an estate sale in Denmark.

"Jorgen sorted through the books, pulled out one and said, 'Here, this one's in English.' You'll never guess what it was!" Nancy exclaimed. "On the inside cover was your name, Dad."

For fifty years I had been separated from my pocket-size Bible. To my delight it had come back to me.

# DAD'S DOG TAGS

*by Lorraine Arents*

————— ⁓⁓ —————

*I*t had been more than three months since my purse
was snatched from me on a New York City street. I had
long since gotten a new purse and wallet, and replaced
my credit cards and driver's license. But even after all
these months, tears still came to my eyes whenever I
thought about the one thing that I could never replace:
my father's dog tags from World War II. I missed Dad
so badly, particularly today as I sat at my desk catching
up on e-mails from friends.

My father had fought on D-Day, helping the
Allied troops establish a bulkhead on the beaches of
Normandy. I was incredibly proud of him, and after
he passed away, I kept his dog tags with me as a reminder of the many sacrifices he had made and the
bravery he had shown.

Every so often, something would make me think of
my father and I would reach in and take those tags out

of my purse. Running my fingers over the engraved letters and numbers, I could almost feel the warmth and strength of Dad's hand clasping mine. Losing those dog tags was almost like losing my father all over again.

Suddenly the phone rang, breaking my reverie. The man on the line introduced himself as the manager at my bank. "Ms. Arents, I've got a police officer here who would like to speak with you," he said.

A police officer? Was I in trouble for something? I wondered.

"I'm glad I was finally able to get ahold of you. Your number was unlisted, so I called your bank," Officer Kraft said. "The manager knew how to get in touch with you. Today on patrol I was inspecting a fence close to the water at Kennedy Airport. Something was stuck on it, covered in seaweed. I looked closer and saw that it was a purse . . ."

My bag! "Was there anything inside?" I asked him, hardly daring to hope.

"Well, yes. Your driver's license, your bank cards . . . and what looks like some old army dog tags," he replied.

"Those tags were my dad's," I said. "He fought at Normandy. I think you were meant to find them today."

"Why?" the officer asked. "What's so special about today?"

"It's June sixth," I said. "D-Day."

# TREASURED ROCKING CHAIR

*by Angie Arthur*

........................... —◊— ...........................

*A* few weeks after Hurricane Katrina hit the Gulf Coast, the Texas school where I teach and my church were collecting furniture and other household items for a family from Louisiana that had lost everything. I thought of how sad it would be to lose all of the things in my house that held so many priceless memories. Nothing could ever really replace a memory. I prayed I would be able to help the Louisiana family in some small way. At least give them practical things they could use.

I had a couple of old chairs in the house, and went into the spare bedroom to dig them out. Then I saw the wooden rocking chair in the corner. Deep brown, with a unique pattern of fruits and leaves stenciled in gold on the back. I'd never seen another like it. I used to rock my son to sleep in it when he was a baby. Talk about memories! I could never bear to part with that rocker.

But a feeling suddenly swept over me. *Give it away.*

"Do you really want to do this?" my husband asked, helping me load the rocking chair into our SUV. "Doesn't it hold sentimental value for you?"

I couldn't explain it. "I just feel like I have to," I told him.

I took the rocker to the school the next day. The woman in charge of the donations for the Louisiana family loaded it into the back of her truck. I hated to see the rocking chair go, but at the same time, I knew somehow that it was the right thing to do.

The very next day at school, the woman in charge came rushing into my classroom. "Angie, I have to tell you a story about that rocking chair!" she said.

The family was grateful for every single item we'd donated, they told her. Then they saw the rocker. Everyone stopped and stared. Then the granddaughter cried out, "Grandma, look! It's your rocking chair!"

The fruits and leaves, stenciled in gold, the dark-brown wood. My rocking chair was exactly like the one they had lost in the hurricane. The one that held their sweetest memories.

# LITTLE BRIAN

*by Lynda Jamison*

—————

*I* couldn't wait to have a baby of my own. My husband, Bob, and I had been trying since we got married a year earlier. Meanwhile, I was volunteering at an adoption home where I helped look after hundreds of babies who were waiting for permanent families.

I cared about all of them, but one blond boy named Brian stole my heart. Brian was underweight and cried all the time. Most of the staff members could do nothing to comfort him, but in my arms, he was calm and quiet. Only there could he fall asleep.

It was obvious Brian would need a very special home. A big part of me wanted that home to be with Bob and me, but the timing was wrong. I heard a family was ready to adopt Brian at about the same time I found out I was pregnant. *Let him be going to good people who'll love him as much as I do*, I prayed when I said good-bye to Brian.

I gave birth to a son and another soon after. With each of their milestones—first step, first word, first day of school—my thoughts turned to Brian. I could only pray he was doing as well. After seven years, I could still see his sweet face clearly in my mind.

One evening my husband and I were invited to have dinner at the home of a couple we had met through a prayer network, and whom we hoped to get to know better. Paul and Maggie invited us in, and I looked around their beautiful home. My eye fell on a baby picture hanging on the wall. I gasped. "That's Brian!"

Maggie came over to my side. "That's our son, Christopher," she said, nodding at the picture. "But he was called Brian when we adopted him. How could you have known that?"

I poured out my story. Then a blond boy in pajamas padded into the room. The baby who couldn't stop crying had grown into a boy with an irresistible smile. In an instant he was in my arms again.

Paul and Maggie became our dearest friends and Christopher like another son to me. I sang at his wedding, and one year later, I held his new baby in my arms.

# Shocking Revelation

*by Gary Klahr*

———∿∿———

Steve Barbin and I first got to talking one night in 1975 when we ended up at tables next to each other at a local restaurant. By the time we finished our burgers, we'd pushed our tables together and were well on the way to becoming best friends. We grew so close that we finished each other's sentences and shared belly laughs at jokes that no one else seemed to get. Even the rhythms of our speech seemed identical. At his wedding, I told Steve he was truly my brother.

Of course, that was just a figure of speech. My parents had tried for years to have a child before I came along, and they called me their gift from God. Steve, on the other hand, was adopted. It was hard to imagine, but he'd known it for years, and told me he'd grown up in a lovely family.

Then, out of the blue in December 1998, I got a phone call from a woman with the Connecticut

Department of Children and Families. She confirmed my name and birth date. "You should probably sit down before I tell you why I'm calling," she said. "Did you know that you were adopted?"

"Are you sure you have the right Gary Klahr?" I asked.

But she persisted. "Believe me, I wouldn't do this if I weren't sure. One of your biological siblings needs urgent medical information from family."

I was floored. My parents always treated me like I was their own child, never once saying I was adopted. They'd wanted to protect me, I guess.

"In all of my years in this work, I've never seen a case like this," she went on. "Your biological parents lived in Bridgeport. They had thirteen children, and nine of them were adopted by other families. Is there someone besides your parents you can talk to about this? Someone you're close to?"

"My buddy Steve is adopted, and he's okay with it," I said slowly. "So I guess I will be too, once I have some time to get over it."

"What's Steve's last name?" she asked.

"Barbin," I said.

"Gary, Steve is your brother."

# Finding Missy

### by Tammy Gardiner

My boyfriend, Wayne, and I, along with my older sisters, Sherry and Deb, were headed up I-275 from our home in St. Petersburg, Florida, to the small town of Hudson that July morning. It was only an hour's drive and I should've been counting down the minutes until we arrived. This was the moment I'd prayed for, reuniting with my little sister, Missy, after thirty years. On my lap I held photos of us—celebrating her eighth birthday, eating pizza with everything on it, me pushing her in her wheelchair. Sherry held her old teddy bear. My stomach was in knots. I wasn't sure Missy wanted to see me. What if all these years she'd blamed me for being taken from our family?

Missy was born when I was five. She had severe cerebral palsy and needed constant attention. Our mother spent most of her time with her boyfriend, working on cars in our front yard and drinking. Deb and Sherry had long left home. It fell to me to care for Missy the best I could, and by the time I turned twelve it was all I did outside of school.

But I cherished the responsibility. Every weekday I woke her in the tiny bedroom we shared, gave her a bath, made her eggs or cereal, and pushed her wheelchair to the bus that took her to her special school near our Tampa Bay town. Afternoons we spent at the park or doing simple puzzles together. The smallest things made her happy and when she broke out in that joyful laugh of hers, I felt like everything was right with the world. I was her best friend and her protector. Most of all I loved Missy and I couldn't imagine life without her. Even now I remembered those days so clearly . . .

Two girls lying in their beds waiting for sleep to come. I looked over at Missy snuggling with her teddy bear and knew she was waiting for me to tell her our favorite story. "When we get older I'm going to buy us a farm," I said. "It'll be beautiful, with acres of land as far as we can see. There'll be ponds with fish and we'll have horses and live together in a log cabin. I'll always take care of you."

But it was a dream that wasn't to be. One day when I was fourteen a woman knocked on the door. "Is there a Missy Gardiner who lives here?" she asked. She said a teacher at Missy's school had reported seeing ants in her wheelchair and that Missy needed to come with her.

"You're not taking my kid," Mom said. But moments later I stood sobbing by the screen door watching the woman push Missy to her car.

When they were gone, Mom turned to me. "This wouldn't have happened if you'd taken better care of her." Missy returned for a short visit in the weeks after that. Then I never saw her again.

I had to get out of there, away from my mom and the house that seemed so empty now. A year later I hopped a bus to New York. All I took with me were some clothes and photos. I struggled, and slowly made a life on my own. But I couldn't escape the pain and guilt I felt over losing Missy. I begged the Lord for a sign that she was being cared for. Nothing. I wondered if God even heard me. Twelve years ago, with Mom showing signs of dementia, I moved back to the Tampa area. I got a house in St. Petersburg near the stadium of my favorite NFL team, the Tampa Bay Buccaneers. I made peace with Mom before she died, but she couldn't tell me what had happened to Missy. Sherry and I found her old teddy bear when we were cleaning out Mom's room at the nursing home, a bittersweet keepsake. Sometimes I thought about trying to find Missy on my own, but I didn't know where to begin. So many years had gone by. It scared me to think about what I might find.

Then Saturday the most amazing thing happened. Betty, my best friend from middle school, and I had just reconnected on Facebook. We'd made plans to drive to another friend's wedding together. Wayne and I got in Betty's car and she handed me a laminated photo from a newspaper. "I've had this for ten years," Betty said, "hoping I might see you again someday."

I looked at the picture, a young smiling woman in a wheelchair, an athletic-looking man next to her. The caption read: Missy Gardiner, a resident of The Angelus in Hudson, was thrilled to meet former Oakland Raiders player Roman Gabriel III . . .

Could it be? My hand was trembling so hard I almost dropped the photo. *Dear Lord, have You answered my prayer?*

"I figured you'd want to have that," Betty said. "'Course you probably see Missy all the time now."

"I . . . I haven't seen her in thirty years," I stammered. "I didn't even know if she was alive."

Betty looked at me, stunned. "I had no idea," she said.

How I wanted to go to Missy right then! But she was obviously at a facility. I couldn't just drop in unannounced. I'd need to call and make an appointment. When we got home I was too nervous to pick up the phone. Wayne finally called The Angelus. We learned it was a residential care center for people with cerebral palsy. The director, Joe Neri, agreed to meet with us, but Wayne said he'd sounded leery. "I'm afraid your visit might confuse Missy," he'd told Wayne. "I need to warn you that she won't remember her sister."

Now, with each passing mile on the interstate, those words were like a drumbeat in my head.

What was I trying to prove? It had been too long. Missy wouldn't recognize me. I hadn't recognized her from her photo until I read the caption. Wasn't it enough just to know that she was healthy and happy? It was too late to turn back the clock or make foolish childhood dreams come true.

We turned off the interstate onto Florida Highway 589. "How much farther?" I asked Wayne.

"About a half hour more," he said, reaching over and taking my hand for a moment. "Don't worry. It's going to be okay."

How could he be sure? What if seeing us confused Missy or, worse, upset her? What if she simply refused to see me? Other than a ten-year-old photo, I knew very little about The Angelus or Missy's care. How long had she been there? Would it be a gloomy kind of place with dark hallways lined with sad, ignored patients?

We turned off the highway down a curvy, wooded road. It seemed isolated and I could feel my stomach tightening even more. Where is this place? We took a right, another right, and a left. Finally, the road opened up and we were there. The Angelus, a sign read by the entrance. We drove down a long winding lane, parked outside the main building, went inside and asked for Joe Neri. He escorted us to a large meeting room and we sat down. My heart was pounding. Joe looked across the table at us, like he was thinking about how to say something.

"Thirty years ago," Joe said, "my mom had a dream of starting a farm for at-risk children. She took a class to prepare for that. In class she met two women who ran a home for mentally handicapped children. They'd brought a girl in a wheelchair they said the state had dumped on them. But she required more care than they could provide. They were going to put her in a state mental institution.

"My mom looked into that little girl's eyes and something touched her soul. She made some calls and discovered there were no facilities for people with cerebral palsy. She decided to turn that farm into a home for them. That girl was Missy and today we have thirty-five residents. The Angelus wouldn't be here if it wasn't for her."

I took Wayne's hand and squeezed it hard, this news almost more than I could absorb. I was glad that

Missy's life had touched so many others, but it didn't lessen my anxiety.

"You see, to Missy, we are her family," Joe said. "I haven't told her yet that you were coming. I didn't think she would understand." He stood up. "Wait here while I get her."

The wait was agonizing and I filled it with prayer.

Finally Joe reappeared pushing a woman in a wheelchair. Her hair was cut very short and she was nicely dressed in a salmon-pink top and khakis. But she looked nothing like the girl I once knew.

"This is Tammy, your sister," Joe told Missy. "You knew her when you were little and she's come to see you."

Missy's eyes were fixed on the floor.

I didn't know what to say. Once it had been so easy to talk to her. Now we were strangers.

"Missy's a big football fan. Aren't you, Missy?" Joe said. "Especially the Buccaneers." She nodded, glancing up shyly at me.

"You're kidding," I said. "Me too. I live right by the stadium. Let me guess, you love pizza with everything on it." She nodded harder. Then she laughed, that big joyful sound I'd waited so many years to hear again.

Sherry reached out and set the teddy bear on her lap. "This is yours," I said. "We've been keeping him for you, but now he wants to stay here with you." Our eyes met and for a second I thought I saw the faintest glimmer of recognition.

"Would you like to show me around?" I said. "I'd love to see where you live." She nodded. I took the handles of her wheelchair and pushed. It felt so natural to be connected to Missy again. Wayne opened the door and we went out onto a paved walkway under a canopy of trees, past a barn with two miniature horses and a pond filled with koi. In the distance I saw the gentle rise and fall of the surrounding fields. They seemed to go on forever. I couldn't believe it! Missy had made it to our farm!

"You know we used to share a room," I said. "I used to tell you stories every night." We went up a slight grade and there at the top, tucked in a small grove of trees, was a log cabin. Just like I'd promised her . . .

We had followed such different paths these past thirty years. Only God could have brought us back together to this spot. It was our childhood dream come to life, except the Lord had taken even better care of Missy than I could have. I rested my hand on my sister's shoulder. Back when we were kids, I couldn't imagine my life without her. Now I didn't have to. I knew we would never again be apart.

# A NOTE
# FROM THE EDITORS

We hope you enjoy *Mysterious Ways: Extraordinary Wonders*, created by the Books and Inspirational Media Division of Guideposts, a nonprofit organization. In all of our books, magazines and outreach efforts, we aim to deliver inspiration and encouragement, help you grow in your faith, and celebrate God's love in every aspect of your daily life.

Thank you for making a difference with your purchase of this book, which helps fund our many outreach programs to the military, prisons, hospitals, nursing homes and schools. To learn more, visit Guideposts Foundation.org.

We also maintain many useful and uplifting online resources. Visit Guideposts.org to read true stories of hope and inspiration, access OurPrayer network, sign up for free newsletters, download free e-books, join our Facebook community, and follow our stimulating blogs.

To learn about other Guideposts publications, including our best-selling devotional *Daily Guideposts*, go to ShopGuideposts.org, call (800) 932-2145 or write to Guideposts, PO Box 5815, Harlan, Iowa 51593.